EAST BATON ROUGE PARISH LIBRARY

Presented by
East Baton Rouge Parish
Library Staff

In memory of
Mary Catherine Terry

Good Measure

Other Books by Robert Morgan

Poetry

Zirconia Poems

Red Owl

Land Diving

Trunk & Thicket

Groundwork

Bronze Age

At the Edge of the Orchard Country

Sigodlin

Green River: New and Selected Poems

Fiction

The Blue Valleys

The Mountains Won't Remember Us

Good Measure

essays, interviews, and notes on poetry

Robert Morgan

Louisiana State University Press

Baton Rouge and London

02 01 00 99 98 97 96 95 94 93   5 4 3 2 1

Designer: Amanda McDonald Key
Typeface: Times
Typesetter: G & S Typesetters, Inc.
Printer and binder: Thomson-Shore, Inc.

Library of Congress Cataloging-in-Publication Data

Morgan, Robert, 1944–
    Good measure : essays, interviews, and notes on poetry / Robert
Morgan.
    p. cm.
    ISBN 0-8071-1798-6
    1. Morgan, Robert, 1944–   —Interviews.   2. Poets, American—20th
century—Interviews.   3. Poetry—Authorship.   4. Poetics.
I. Title.
PS3563.087147Z466   1993
814'.54—dc20
                                                                    92-34860
                                                                    CIP
The essays and other pieces herein were previously published as follows, sometimes under slightly different titles, and are reprinted by permission: "Some Sentences on the Line," *Epoch,* XXXIX (Winter, 1980), 207–209; "Good Measure," *Epoch,* XXXIII (Fall–Winter, 1983), 80–81; "The Cubist of Memory," *The Generation of 2000,* ed. William Heyen (Princeton, N.J., 1984), 191–94; "Poetry and Revival," *Bluefish,* II, No. 3/4, 75–78; "Asylum of the Real," *Mississippi Review,* XIX (1991), 90–91; "The Gift of Pause," *Cream City Review,* XV (Fall–Winter, 1991), 21–23; "Bryant's Solitary Glimpse of Paradise," *Under Open Sky,* ed. Norbert Krapf (New York, 1986), 56–57; "Robinson Jeffers: Eye and Fountain," *American Poetry,* V (Fall, 1987), 90; "Insect, Bowl, Horizon," *Epoch,* XXVIII (Spring–Summer, 1979), 299–304; "The Kingdom of Childhood," Introduction to Jean Follain, *Canisy,* trans. Louise Guiney (Durango, Colo., 1982), xi–xix; "The Compound Vision of A. R. Ammons' Early Poems," *Epoch,* XXII (Spring, 1973), 343–63; "The Toy-Maker's Closet," *Bluefish,* I, No. 1, 9–25; "The Transfigured Body: Notes from a Journal," *The Small Farm,* No. 3 (1976), 31–39; "Mica: Reflective Bits from Notebooks," *Seneca Review,* XXI (Fall, 1991), 152–57; "Interview by Jeff Daniel Marion," *The Small Farm,* No. 3 (1976), 40–43; "Interview by Suzanne Booker," *Carolina Quarterly,* XXXVII (Spring, 1985), 13–22; "The Rush of Language: Interview by William Heyen and Stanley Rubin," *The Post-Confessionals,* ed. Stanley Rubin *et al.* (Rutherford, N.J., 1988), 197–209; "Conversation with William Harmon," *Iron Mountain Review,* VI (Spring, 1990), 11–16. "Fred Chappell's *Midquest*" was first published in *American Poetry Review,* XI (1982), 45–47.

Extracts from poems by A. R. Ammons are reprinted from *Collected Poems, 1951–1971,* by A. R. Ammons, by permission of W. W. Norton & Company, Inc. Copyright © 1972 by A. R. Ammons. Extracts from Russell Edson's poems are reprinted from Russell Edson, *The Clam Theater* ("The Broken Daughter," "Pinocchio's Bride"), copyright 1973 by Russell Edson, and *Why the Closet-Man Is Never Sad* ("The Double Bed," "The Parental Decision," "The Reason Why the Closet-Man Is Never Sad," "The Rooming House Dinner"), copyright 1977 by Russell Edson, from Wesleyan University Press by permission of University Press of New England. Extracts from poems by Fred Chappell are taken from *Midquest,* copyright 1981 by Fred Chappell, and are reprinted by permission of Louisiana State University Press.

The author would like to thank the John Simon Guggenheim Memorial Foundation, the National Endowment for the Arts, the New York Foundation for the Arts, and the Rockefeller Foundation Bellagio Study Center for support while writing portions of this book.

Contents

I

language that counts

Some Sentences on the Line

1980

The force of the line is sinister, rushing always out of the left, as language or speech originates from the left side of the brain, into the virgin space of the right. We have the sense of moving constantly, in the line as in the whole poem, from the curious and ambiguous to structure, recognition.

My first confident sense of reading poetry came with the discovery that Eliot's *Four Quartets* were made of strong sentences folded into line forms. Before that I remember being too intimidated by rhymed stanzas to try anything more than prose squibs and Sandburg-like snatches of dialogue.

My first principle of versification was, Make something happen in every line. Each line should be an entering of new territory, in the ongoing momentum of the poem. Each line is an image, an increment of energy.

The line builds suspense toward the realization of turning in midspeech to the next line, and allows us to create verbal surprises. Most lines are a gathering of force, a staging ground for the flight to the next.

Line length is a way of speeding or slowing the poem's current, as with resistors and condensers. Long lines read faster than short because the line, like a pendulum swing, tends to have the same duration no matter how many words it contains. The line is the basic unit of fragmentation of the sentence whereby we can magnify or slip over a passage to direct attention. It is one of our most effective ways of measuring out the delivery of idea, image, perceptual energy. To keep the forwarding motion, some lines should be run-on. Lines are the grid marks on which the tangles of goal-seeking action are played out, where each play is a new beginning.

We need horizontal contrast to the poem's movement down the page, and use the line for that purpose. The line can be seen as the balance pole for the high-tension strut and tumble of the poem.

The best lines please and stimulate through counterpointing eye and ear. We see the line come to a stop but hear the voice continue. The visual impact creates a paradox with the aural. Someone has compared the movement of a poem through its lines to the way groundwater hunts among pebbles and trash for a way down, sometimes pausing to fill a depression or back away from a dead end, then rushing a needle down steepness, but always in motion, always fluent and arriving, and accurate through tortuous and irregular forms to the forces calling it on.

Lineation can be called a labanotation for the voice, or a choreography for eye movement across the page. The white spaces between lines and at either end suggest the silence running back millions of light-years against which the poem is spoken.

The prose poem is an interesting but legendary form. Its best practitioners, such as Russell Edson, are usually specialized fictionalists, storytellers. Few contemporary poets have a consistent practice of the line. We lament the absence of a defining orthodoxy, and celebrate the pluralism and heterodoxy, admitting we need more excellence, fewer technicalities, less explanation. We want the authority of inspired originality and the authority of ancient form at once, and honor the paradox with vernacular lyricism.

We should find in true lines a touch of alpenglow, as though they reach far enough to reflect light we cannot always see. Lean regular lines should act as a neutral screen through which we suddenly see a drama taking place, near focus on word and detail leading to deep focus on action, and the immobility beyond action.

I like poems in fragments, things with rough and sharp edges that sometimes cut unexpectedly, that cannot be handled too easily and always with safety. One piece of broken quartz can shave an ax handle, same as an expensive plane. Lines are the gathered bits of the original shattered diamond. I like the idea that by breaking sentences into lines we can have something of crystalline perfection in the living voice. Motion and stillness at once.

Good Measure

1983

The formal decisions made while writing a poem are usually forgotten soon as enacted. It is only the poem we want to remember, whether written in one or fifty drafts. So many choices in composition are made unconsciously, almost by reflex, and many of the happiest touches in a poem are accidents, gifts of the gods of chance. All poets are hopeless gamblers.

Grandma's Bureau

Shivering and hoping no one
would come from the heated rooms, I
handled the great black comb fine as
the sieve of a whale's mouth, and dared
not look at the coffin-wardrobe.
My finger bulldozed dust on wood
and left a half-moon of lint at
the end of its trail. The steel brush
held a few gray strands among its
thousand stingers. My breath summoned
a ghost to the heavy pane of
the tortoiseshell mirror. More than
all I loved to slide the hatpins
like adjustable rods in the
plum-shaped cushion. They pushed out and
in like throttles and chokes of some
delicate engine. There was a
mystery to such thin strength. I
knew without asking I wouldn't be
allowed such deadly probes and heart-
picks. Some were long as witches' wands
with fat pearl heads. They slid in the

cushion as through waxy flesh.
I extracted a cold sliver
excalibur and ran it on
my wrist and stabbed at the mirror,
then froze, listening for her steps.

"Grandma's Bureau" represents much of the work I have been doing recently. The versification is the simplest I know, an eight-syllable line with no regular meter, no counting of stresses. It is almost-free verse broken into an arbitrary length, based vaguely on four-beat common meter: a kind of humble blank verse. I like this form because it leaves the musical cadence almost entirely free to follow the content, the narrative line, the local dynamics of the sentence, yet has some of the surface tension of regularity, the expectation of repetition, with the fulfillment and surprises of advancement across an uneven terrain.

My greatest difficulty here, in fitting the sentences into lines, has been avoiding too many articles and conjunctions at the ends of lines. A few final *the*s and *and*s create a run-on effect that helps the narration; too many seem like half-justified prose. When I can, I like to retain the autonomy of each line, making it an increment of energy, a self-sufficient image or forwarding of thought, earning its own way. (Or as I used to say, Make something happen in every line.) The music of poetry is not of the metronome, but can be as free as Webern or Stravinsky. A truism now, but an enabling recognition when I was twenty. Suddenly it seemed possible to write in lines and say something, more than in prose, and I began to hammer out my first rough verses.

Giving good measure means that we always deliver more than is expected, more than is required by our contract with the reader. It is the unexpected abundance that delights most, the bonus that could not have been foreseen. Besides good faith, the good measure of the voice gives assurance and reassurance, control, accuracy, direction. Its music turns and enlivens time. The good measure of poetry is the finding of the true response, the appropriate gesture that fits word and experience into a whole. Poetry measures in essential heartbeat the enactment of knowledge through the saying out. The stave is tailored to experience, and sets experience. A poem unexpectedly confides the significant secret.

It is the willingness to address the elementary and elemental that makes a voice interesting. A random fact triggers the memory of the telling detail. When we see the familiar from several unexpected angles at once, the music seems to go right of its own accord.

In the body of the poem, lineation is part flesh and part skeleton, as form is the towpath along which the burden of content, floating on the formless, is pulled. All language is both mental and sacramental, is not "real" but is the working of lip and tongue to subvert the "real." Poems empearl irritating facts until they become opalescent spheres of moment, not so much résumés of history as of human faculties working with pain. Every poem is necessarily a fragment empowered by its implicitness. We sing to charm the snake in our spines, to make it sway with the pulse of the world, balancing the weight of consciousness on the topmost vertebra.

The Cubist of Memory

1984

You begin with a vision of making something glorious, then fumble for a way of realizing that unheard music. I remember staring across the Green River valley in western North Carolina toward Cicero Mountain when about fourteen and thinking that the summit seemed woolly and domed as a mastodon heaving itself out of the west into morning. I wanted to make a "poem" as grand as the mountain, as voluptuous as its flanks, as remote and lofty, yet fertile with springs and cliffs and mold-fed vegetation. January seepage over the peak cliff froze and glistened like a single diamond eye. Until I studied piano at nine or ten and learned to read notes, I often heard music in my thoughts while looking out on ridge or pasture, or jerking up weeds, or sitting in prayer meeting. The long compositions I made up mentally were based on hymns and snatches of organ and orchestral music heard on my grandfather's radio. Every fact and landscape and time seemed to have its melodic correlative.

After a long circuit through science and math—those were "beat the Russians" years—I came back to music through storytelling. I drafted many stories and pieces of novels in my late teens at Chapel Hill, and even published some of the former. Then I decided that southern fiction had been done already; but southern poetry was nearly nonexistent. I would go off in an unknown direction, away from Faulknerian rhetoric toward plainness, compactness, simplicity. I wanted a clean transparent music, nonmetrical, experimental, "classical." To help free myself from myself—from ego, ambition, self-consciousness—to get on with the work, I tried to be true to objects, and to the verbal objects that measured and enacted world and thought. I wanted poems terse and precise, yet encompassing as mathematical proofs.

When my sister brought her freshman anthology home from Bob Jones University I read in it the opening section of "Song of Myself" and was astonished and exhilarated that one could leap in a sentence from the soul to a single spear of grass. I also found there Wallace Stevens' "Domination of Black" and remember a similar elation at the colors, and the comparison of leaves turning like the fire with the gathering of planets. The combination of intimacy and distance was unforgettable. But my prose squibs and haiku and images never became poems, the breath of poems, until I realized that poems were voice, were telling sentences.

"Cedar" was written in the summer of 1970 when I was exploring the most elemental kinds of poems. I began a series on metals, and finished one called "Copper." I would choose the name or image of something common and try to describe it accurately, and then evoke the associations brought to mind. "Cedar" was more successful than most, I think, because I got the sound right. The longer, sustained sentences integrate the levels of reference and metaphor. As I remember, the seed of the poem was the idea of likeness and unlikeness, wood becoming music, sap becoming scent, the finite expanding infinitely. All senses echoed, as Baudelaire said, and all images and memories were kin. All were in some fantastic way equal: beauty and ugliness, absence and presence, the significant and useless. The ear knows long before the mind whether a poem or passage is working. It is music that tells the meaning. But also, it is the meaning that makes the music. The tune of poetry comes more from what is said, and how quickly it is said, than from stresses and rests. Economy tends to create melody. My dream was to write a maquette-sized poetry, of bonsai complexity and detail. Each poem was a new beginning of perception, an atom of recognition, explosive in its transfers of bond and structure.

"Pumpkin," written January 18, 1972, during my first year at Cornell, shows the same preoccupation with description. Starting out to render pumpkins buried under weeds I came upon the planets rising. I have been asked why the title is singular, and have no good answer, except to say "Pumpkin" was the working title and seemed to evoke the essence of the thing, something more mythic than "Pumpkins." I like the feeling of homemadeness in a poem, the thing jotted and joined from materials at hand. A poet can travel light because his resources are the landscape and language he travels through, which mirror those he carries within.

"Face" (1974) shows my growing interest in the use of conversational tone and narrative. Coming to Cornell and talking daily with students and colleagues changed, apparently, my sense of cadence. I could write in longer units. Where before my poems had seemed to be spoken against the silence of all eternity, they began to sound more like someone talking on a given afternoon. I had been especially terrified, when young, of Jesus coming again and taking all but me to heaven. It was not Blake's tiger I had in mind, but Eliot's "Christ the tiger." I am only now realizing the importance of hymns and gospel songs to me, both their words and their music: for the sense of far-off heaven, of revival, sadness, submission, of ecstatic promise of resurrection. The central figure of our culture is that promise of rebirth. The stuff of poetry is compost, human as well as vegetable, verbal and cultural; but it is the prospect of rising from the rot and ruin that empowers the statement and embodiment of the words.

In the mid-1970s I discovered not only narrative in verse, and the wealth of loric material in my family memories, but also rhymed forms and balladic horror and compression. The best of these experiments were probably "Wedding Party" and "Mountain Bride." The latter is based on a story I heard my grandfather tell by the fireplace. I thought he must have known those Revises, since there were Revises in our community. But when I read the poem at UNC-Asheville a member of the audience mentioned that John Ehle had told the same story in one of his novels, and later I found it was a widely known folktale. I hope I have added something to it by condensation, selection of detail, and form.

"Buffalo Trace." Among my favorite writers are Bartram, Alexander Wilson, Audubon, André Michaux, Lewis and Clark. I like the sense that the continent has been written on by glaciers, earthquakes, floods, buffalo, Indians, and hunters. The soil is haunted by the Cherokee and Iroquois, extinct giant animals, ice tracks, frontier preachers. Looking for new ground to clear we find Old Fields, scrublands opened by fire or ice storms or Indian hoe-farmers. All is in fragments, and the recognition and gathering of those shards inspire the cubism of memory and imagination that implies the whole. All the best poetry is fragments joined in new ways, the broken edges sharp enough to cut as well as refract light and attention. At our best we recognize that we are just members of the chorus of language, that our voices, when most our own, are in concert with speakers past and present, with facts and their metaphorical fables.

Reflecting the rivers and oceans of buffalo were the streams and inland seas of birds, the passenger pigeons. No image in all the early travel reports evokes the pristine grandeur of the interior more than the descriptions of those extinct hosts. When writing the poem "Passenger Pigeons" I could think of no modern equivalent except air traffic, and TV and radio signals.

In my earliest memories our house is filled with the flotsam and left-overs of World War II. I played with chevron patches, messkits, gas masks brought back by my uncles. The bureau drawer held ration books, and in the button box were several paper penny tokens from 1943. But over all the paraphernalia and talk was the spoken and unspoken presence of my Uncle Robert who had been killed in a B-17 in 1943, the year before I was born. He cast a shadow almost as large as the biblical figures' over my play and daydreams. The pigeons in the attic, the toolboxes and paint set; even my name had been his. I constantly felt the difference between his reported goodness and generosity and my own fear and mischief. He had been an athlete, a martyr, an artist, and I had no choice but to rebel, then follow.

I began writing "Lightning Bug" in 1969, but was unable to find an appropriate ending. Finally the phrase "the edge of the orchard country" came to me this year (1983). It suggested redolence, proximity and dis-tance, a projecting of attention out to the horizon of trees and stars. Sud-denly the poem felt complete, and I could let it rest.

We love poetry in part because it is useless. In an age when everything seems to have its price and schedule, poetry is without deadlines or market value; it is undenominated by party or church or special-interest lobby. Its playfulness both serves and is subversive to causes we solemnly admire. Poetry's power is very real, though indirect. A great poem can affect the lives of all, whether they read it or not. As poetry is based on the gold standard of experience, so experience is keyed to the bedrock of the best expression. My understanding of tradition is that our language and age are writing us, in ways we can't always see. An individual may have nothing better to contribute than a radical, humble attention that both startles and reassures.

Poetry and Revival

1985

Generalizations about poetry are of course easy to make and difficult to make stick. The recognitions and clarifications of one week or decade become the restrictions and clichés of the next. An apparent bull's-eye of critical thought can turn out a complete miss the next time we read or write a poem of any originality.

It is irritating to poets that contemporary criticism has so little to do with "poetry." Theorists may address signs and language and rhetoric in interesting ways, but there seems no point of contact with the concerns of most working poets. I once asked a young theorist who had just spent a year in Paris what current French poetry was like; it was clear from her response that she had never considered the subject. My impression was that poetry in the city of Baudelaire and Apollinaire might be in hiding.

Part of our frustration comes from the very "success" of poetry in our time. Poets may not be on prime-time TV, but never before have there been so many fellowships, prizes, chairs, anthologies, publications. Creative writing has moved into the universities, and we expect some golden age. But in spite of the honors and tenure, good poems are just as difficult to write and find. The only promise ever was for more hard work and the opportunity for still more patience and work of the indirect, lazy, exploratory kind.

We strain under the burden of being "national," but without knowing who is speaking to whom we respond to the pressure not to be "regional" or "parochial" with a kind of faultless blandness. Nothing can be universal except by virtue of its accuracy. Nothing can compete for scope with true observation. Poetry that gets too far from fact loses its power of fable also. An important recognition of poetry has always been that the insignificant may be just as fertile to attention as the obviously significant. It is the contrast with vision, the fusing across distance of the two, in which poetry soars. But much of poetry's value is still that it looks at the unnoticed, the unimportant, and discovers there a brightness.

Most of the work published in any age is a kind of "boardwalk poetry." It has the vision of a tourist in language, within sight of the ocean, but above the sand and turmoil, with a view of the bathers, the novelty shops, the crowds on promenade, out of sight of mudflats and fishing wharves. A pleasant, even intelligent poetry, but not an act of discovery or large spirit. If I quarrel with my contemporaries, it is mostly over the stress on the poet above the poetry, and the poetry above poems. I am interested in specific works, and less in the personalities of the poets, and the poetry in general.

One of the charges most often heard against contemporary poetry is that it has no audience, it is written for other poets or, at the very best, for the classroom. It is ironic that the American poet who wanted most to be the bard of the masses, of working folk, of city and countryside, Walt Whitman, had the least popular readership in his own time. His audience was Emerson and his neighbors, the Pre-Raphaelites, the young literati of the eastern cities. But the more scholarly and aristocratic Longfellow was a national hero whose romances and ballads sold by the hundreds of thousands and were memorized by schoolchildren. It is thanks in part to Longfellow and Tennyson that we have the myth of popular poetry. Before the industrial revolution and mass literacy, the audience for poetry was necessarily limited, privileged: those who could read. The new reading middle class of the nineteenth century created a vast market for novels in verse or prose and sentiment in any form, including verse. Because of that success we tend to have the illusion that there was once a golden age when almost everyone read or sang the best words in the best order. But the large audience, that never read poetry anyway, long ago moved on to television, pop music, *People* magazine. Poets need not assume guilt for loss of a readership they never had.

Certainly poetry today is missing the hype of the fifties and sixties, when Ginsberg was often pictured in *Time* and the newspapers, not to mention on national television. Lowell was photographed on the steps of the Pentagon for millions who would never read a line by him. If poets are doing their work more quietly, with fewer radical pretensions, it may be just as well. What poetry has lost in public relations it may have regained in substance.

In the 1960s talk was that poetry readings would expand the audience for poetry, or that the performance of poetry might change and then "replace" the printed text. But the most successful readers were often the weaker poets, and even the better poets often found their best poems didn't work well on the platform. At least one poet I knew of had a separate body of work for readings and another for publication. The reading circuits took many poets far from their acknowledged sources in solitude and intense work.

Poetry is rarely forward looking, but is most powerfully retrospective, recollective. Poetry's subject is almost always the imaginative past. Not for nothing was Memory the mother of muses. Too much concern for the merely experimental makes for superficiality. Sometimes a Pasternak can hint of the luminous and lucid future, but that kind of rhetoric is more typical of the Third Reich than of good poetry.

Only art seems able to stand up to and against entropy, catabolism, aging. Against history, cruelty, loss, fear. Our consciousness is so structured it lives best in this trope: seed and season, spore and sun. For poetry says that everything is dying even while it lives, and that dead it will be remembered. The mind, which does not believe that it can die, seizes on both the warning and the promise. All elegy ends with expectation. A poem whispers that, though all is death, and all chants are death chants, there can be no death. It is the only clue that counts. If that sense of recovered truth is not found in the reading, the poem fails to delight. The reader is the exponent that raises attention and memory in the poem to new (and old) powers.

Language is appetency, the revival of desire, to see, taste, to become, to transform. The earth and disease of experience are torn open by the anti-gravity of language. All tropes are variations on the figure of resurrection. Every reading reenacts the essential mystery.

Donald Hall has said, "Words are the sensuous body of pleasure, but content is pain." Notice the passion of his brilliant figure. It is the carnality of language that gives pleasure, but the vexation of meaning provides significance. Without the promise of resurrection we have only the Stoic's wise quietness, the ultimate stage of thought in the classical world, an armor against more pain. But recognizing the grief of experience, there is the possibility of recreation. As Henry Vaughan has it, poetry is "the dead alive and busy."

We want at once the authority of ancient form and the playfulness and freshness of vernacularity, incorporating the unpoetic into poetry. How does one know when the game is played well, when the only guideline is the free verse line? We look for new compromises, openness and closedness at once. Syllabics, rhyme without meter, meter without rhyme, irregular rhyme schemes. All act as flywheels that carry the poem over the threatened stallouts, the pauses and changes of direction, the creek-pool rubato.

My impression is that poetry is thriving in hidden-away places while the great careers come and go. The poets of my generation have suffered from the lack of good teaching from their elders. The previous generation had the great good fortune to go to school to F. O. Matthiessen, Lionel Trilling, R. P. Blackmur, Yvor Winters, Cleanth Brooks, etc. In almost every case they rebelled against their mentors, but had acquired in the meantime both a knowledge and a standard by which to measure themselves.

Still, it is no excuse for us to say that writing programs are bankrupt of serious and imaginative teaching, that the famous and highly paid poets avoid their students, belittle their art, and mock the young with facile response. Overpraise and overprizing always take their toll. If there is a disgrace in the softness of our critical approach, in the flattery and pretense of liking everybody's work, it is no worse than in any other age. Benvenuto Cellini often feared for his life, not from ruffians, but from the pope and great patrons who did not want to pay him. Finishing a work he sometimes had to sneak out of town unpaid. The golden age of Florence was as corrupt, seedy, vicious, obscene as any. What are we waiting for? We have no excuse for not saying the truth with wit, and for not making poems that will shine long after we have ceased our worry and hope.

Asylum of the Real

1991

I'm not sure but what there has always been a feeling of decline about the world of poetry, a sense that contemporary poetry lacks the "vision" and "statement" of the great poets of the past. We think of poetry as an ideal, something so right and true it's virtually unattainable in practice, a gift, a quest. It is the very wonderfulness of poetry that makes us feel such disappointment in the actual results, in the confusions of literary life. This disappointment must be akin to that the devout experience, keenly aware of both the love of God and the pettiness of individuals and institutions.

There is no doubt we currently lack persuasive critics and editors to help sort through the welter and contradictions. As the young theorists have turned increasingly to other concerns poetry has been left in its own ghetto, while prose fiction has been elevated in both the popular press and literary theory. Never has so much ordinary fiction been so lavishly praised and so much good poetry been ignored or blandly reviewed. But it is not surprising that prose fiction should come into its own in an age of greed, corporate takeovers, infinite consumption. The major theme of novels is money, while the major subject of poetry is the recovery of spiritual desire.

Poetry refreshes partly because it is an alternative to the glitz and hurry around us. With poetry there are no deadlines, no blockbusters, no super-agents giving big advances and orders. Poets are free to take their time and do their work right, while no one else is noticing.

I like it that poetry does new things in new vernaculars, different forms and sounds, at the same time it does the very old things, honoring the dead, recognizing mortality, the swing of seasons, naming the ambiguous, soothing the troubled and grieved. All poems have the power of mystery, combining two or more worlds of reference at once. Even the simplest poems function as fanfares and anthems of perception.

I like the way poetry finds brightness in the ordinary and imperfect, the way memory turns out to be prediction. Poetry connects the instant with all times, and irrigates a present that seems otherwise diminished, a prison, a weak imitation of the past.

If much of the best poetry today is being written in the South it is because poets there still have an interest in history, in narrative, in place and landscape. Poetry finds the history implicit in language. Like the periodic chart, a grid of curt, terse signs can imply the whole universe. It is in the instant of passion we are united with all other people. Poetry reminds us of the wisdom of work.

As Emerson deified self, and Stevens deified imagination, our contemporaries have deified language. Paradoxically, the best poetry shows the impoverishment of language as mere language. Poetry begins where criticism ends, recognizing the limits and frustrations of language. The war between philosophy and poetry is natural, extending at least back to Socrates and forward to today's semiotician.

American poetry seems to happen in the most unexpected places, ignored by all until occasions of national emergency or crisis, when we are proud someone has found words appropriate to our mourning.

Science gives us new vocabularies, images, figures. Schrödinger is to us what Aquinas was to Dante. But the ends of poetry and science are still very different.

I like it that poetry is the one literary art that doesn't seem to need a large audience. One or two readers or listeners will do. A popular audience for poetry is a popular illusion.

Many young critics are reluctant to write about poetry because it is so elusive, and subversive to orthodoxies of political correctness. Through their rituals and mystery poems relocate the asylum of the real, the theaters of the natural. The art of the lyric is a process of distortion and accuracy, making the little big, the vast minute, the far near, the familiar strange.

In every age the institutions of poetry seem to stand between the poets and their potential audience. The institutions must focus on the art of the past, for they cannot know the present. When verse can no longer express the grief and glory of being, the history and narratives of character, place, hope, the energy of poetry will pass into other forms and media. But so far no other form has offered the compression, the intensity and intimacy, the memorability of verse.

The Gift of Pause

1991

Sometimes I suspect that poets are far more interested in literary theory than theorists are interested in poetry. Since the early 1970s literary critics and theorists have pretty much abandoned poetry. But I also suspect that in the long run the theory debates of the present will have little influence on poetry. Poetry, historically, has shown a remarkable ability to go its own way in spite of philosophical and academic controversy. An example would be the philosophical wars that raged between the Thomists of Paris and the nominalists of Oxford in the fourteenth century and beyond. For several generations the schoolmen attacked and defended grand syntheses and skeptical deconstructions. It seemed a revolution was going on in the universities and in the European intellectual community. Yet one would be hard pressed to find much evidence of the controversy in the poetry of Chaucer or *Sir Gawain and the Green Knight*, both written at that time. Both poets were deeply concerned with philosophical issues, but apparently not with what seemed to many the central debate of the century.

For reasons not entirely clear poetry has seemed especially elusive to contemporary theory. Third-rate novels, the soap operas of the 1840s, seem more useful to many theorists of American culture than the poetry of Emerson. Literary quality is no consideration. This lack of interest in quality among critics has left poets even more in the academic niche of creative writing. And poets seem to have returned the favor. Only the worst poetry of our time seems to directly connect with literary theory.

The truth is poetry begins where much theorizing ends, with a sense of the difficulty, deception, arbitrariness of language. It is that very evasiveness and ambiguity with which the poet constructs the powerful text. The difficulty and elusiveness are some of the tools of the imagination. The theorist seems to deify language, then declare it dead. But the poet respects, fears, courts, and learns from language. Poets, however assured, even arrogant, they may seem in person, work in humility to the medium, learning and accepting what they are given, by language, by other humans, by nature.

Poetry is the source of all other writing. Language was discovered by and for poetry, for the delight of naming and saying. Language is not essentially utilitarian, but a medium of playfulness and reassurance. It is a social instrument, but its very basis is metaphor, naming one thing in terms of another. We are all poets to some extent in sharing that delight and recognition of just naming. The one thing all poets share, and probably all theorists too for that matter, is a common love for the use of language.

It is probable that a culture that does not love and respect nature will not care much for poetry. Nature is to a large extent still the universal language, and therefore the language of poetry. But poets may see nature as theater, as threat, as text and narrative. Nature is ritual, both mystery and fact.

Though poetry may have lost much of its narrative concern over the years to fiction and film, there are still certain celebrations that only poetry can perform. The concerns of fiction are formidable and related to poetry. And the concerns of film are poetic, visual and quick, but neither is meditative, implicit, off to the side yet rising to the power of statement in the way poetry is.

Poetry's greatest gift is pause. Poetry travels calendar-wise and otherwise. Its best reach is across time, beyond fashions. It partakes of permanence, and sees the otherworldliness in this one. Poetry's greatest power is to suggest an ideal, a quest, something not completely realizable. It is the perfect crystal lattice of language grown on the solution of prose, in the welter of memory and observation, repression and desire. The test of poetry is the sense of rightness, the inevitability of its alignment and sequence.

Form is poetry's destiny and freedom. Only through the poise of form can a poem resist and contain the turbulence of experience.

Poets live in terror of not being able to write again. They spend their day waiting for the mail, and waiting for the next poem. Because the best poems are given, as well as made, poets spend much of their lives trying to balance impatience with desire, humility with aspiration, resistance with confidence.

Politicization of poetry can inspire poets, but more often it forces them to poses, to prove how correct, how sensitive they are, how enlightened. The result is superficial. Poetry is too visceral, written from the guts and genes, and from deepest memory, to be amenable to such programs. Poetry will not fall in line for denomination or platform.

Contemporary theory has been most interesting for poets in the way it has challenged the canons of literature. For a poet the canon is always in flux, always adjusting and distorting itself. One of the exciting things about studying poetry over a long period of time is the pleasure of tracking the shifts in taste and definition. Science progresses over the ages, poetry circles and soars.

The power of statement is essential to the greatest poetry. Fiction is always specific, always particular. Poetry moves between the poles of quiddity and haecceity, and derives much of its power from that movement, that sense of recognition and arrival.

The current balkanization of American poetry accurately reflects the fragmentation of our society. To some extent free verse is responsible for losing poetry its audience, but it was the fashion for theory that lost poetry its critical community.

I sometimes think that only a charismatic figure could revive a popular interest in poetry. Forty years ago the celebrity of Dylan Thomas, his reading tours across the country and back, sparked a revival of interest in poets and poetry that grew over the next two decades and finally petered out in the 1970s. I can remember the faces of Berryman, Lowell, and Ginsberg on the covers of *Time* and *Life* in the 1960s.

On the other hand, much of the best poetry has been written out of the way, in an isolated corner while nobody was looking. And it is only years later that the poetry of a Blake or Dickinson or Hopkins is discovered and cherished. It is one of the wonders of poetry that it happens in such intense privacy and then reverberates in the stadium of the future, twenty years, two hundred years later.

It is not useful to accuse theorists of being the inside traders of criticism and literature of the 1980s, of taking over the fields and dismantling them for the sake of quick careers. The focus and purpose of poetry lie elsewhere.

The best poets write *up* to their audiences, assuming a readership smarter, better informed, more patient and perceptive, than themselves. Only at the moment of making the poem is the poet at his or her best. At the moment of writing poets find within themselves traces of the sublime. Poetry depends less on radical piety than on radical attention. If novel writing is like traveling on a long journey, poem making may be compared to staying still and letting the world and heaven come to you.

II

music's mirror ——————————————————————————————

Bryant's Solitary Glimpse of Paradise

1985

William Cullen Bryant is the first American poet because he is the first to have glanced at Paradise. His Eden is more dignified and classical than the imaginary gardens of Poe, Emerson, Thoreau, Whitman, and Dickinson, but he saw an authentic vision of vast spaces and silence in which a single waterfowl drifted, and forests soughed hymns to be overheard by the solitary, and the ground was haunted and sacred with the memory of primeval dead. Wherever he looked, in his youth, in his best poems, there was the Eden-glimmer that was the essence of our first poetry.

Between the wilderness and the Enlightenment, between the church clearing and the hunting woods, at the edge of the industrial age, Bryant struck his new note. Just when the savage and the true wilderness were almost gone from New England, and the faith that opposed them waning, he glanced into the forest shadows and found dignity and confidence, a stoic joy. Looking closely at the earth around him he saw a moral language of process, consonant with deism, inspiring trust, comfort, in the rational mind.

After the terror and exclusions of Calvinism, what an assurance to see the infinite cycles of decay and growth, incorporating human compost in fertile progression. Most great poems touch somehow the figure of resurrection, but "Thanatopsis" succeeds through its noble music in evoking communion through death and collective loss. The wilderness and nature are death, but mind and imagination are comforted by nature's parallels with deity. Rather than damnation or sainthood, there is the infallible grace of community with all. Eternity and the future are transfigured beneath our feet.

Bryant is the first distinctive American poetic voice, and the first luminist. When he speaks he overcomes inherited fear through elevation and stability, echoing the Romantics, but also glimpsing the freedom and radiance of a new world. He speaks of exhilarating distances, and the thrill of aloneness that Boone and Audubon, Bartram and André Michaux, had known before him. He is the poet of childhood and sunsets, of sowing and orchards, of the homemade line he fashioned from the devotional poems and hymns he was familiar with, and which he subverted to serve his new vision. It is appropriate that he touched his note when young and never found another, for he is the youthful poet of a young country. His best poems seem both old and new at once, reflecting his wise revisions and the rural, half-English world that nurtured him. If his accent still reminds us of Gray and Collins at times, it suggests also the fresh forests and rivers and skies around him, and the gleam of heaven within the transience. The virgin woods flower over the strata of heaped dead in the language, in the reaches of imaginative memory. If his homiletic tone seems wrong to our ears, his observation and music are still accurate. Without its last stanza "To a Waterfowl" may seem a more perfect lyric to our taste, a limpid song of openness and solitude, but it would not be the poem that Bryant meant, and it would not be the sweet vision of poise and aspiration the youthful, somewhat awkward America of his time responded to and loved.

Robinson Jeffers: Eye and Fountain

1987

For no American poet are the facts more contradictory. Famous as the poet of the great rocks and sunlight of the Pacific coast, the landscape at the continent's end, Jeffers was of New England as much as Eliot or any other modern American poet, and he carried the blood of Calvinist preachers in his veins. Though he is our foremost poet of the West, Jeffers has little of the ease or careless informality we associate with California. He is a major influence on contemporary poets, on William Everson and Gary Snyder and the later Roethke, as well as the English Ted Hughes, and yet his work has remained at the margins of the modern canon. It is difficult even today, twenty-three years after his death, to account at once for both the power of his lines and the critical neglect of his poetry. I believe that these paradoxes reflect the uncertainties and disconnections of American culture as well as the contradictions inherent in Jeffers' work. There are disjunctions in his poems that will always hamper a complete acceptance or appreciation, while the splendors of his voice and vision will call us back to read him year after year.

Reading Jeffers I have been struck by how he has refound "the mighty line" of Whitman and Melville. His language rages and breaks over the reader with a force rarely found in modernist poetry. He writes at the wavelength of ocean and coast range, plunging cliffs. And through the dignity of that heavy line we hear a love of the thrill of mortality and evil in the world, a love of both tragic and natural grandeur. Toward the end of his life he seemed to be in love with death, but in most of his poems there is a love of the forms of nature, and a love of his hatred for things human.

Though Jeffers may sound like a Calvinist, a preacher, an Old Testament prophet, he has the confidence and faith in nature of a pantheist. This is one reason his poetry finally seems strange. The rage of the voice is at odds with the vision of an eternal nonhuman world. He is certainly not a poet of Self, or "imperial self," autobiography, confession. For him inanimate nature is the very image of God, and reality the thoughts of God. Rock and sea, hawk and sun, are the flesh and mind of deity. Redwood and ocean are the scripture he reads and quotes for his sermons. And the evil in the world to which he alludes, and the depravities his vision assumes, are never as real to the reader as the details of nature he evokes. His anti-humanism, or ahumanism, seems undercut by the serenity and beauty around him, and by the peacefulness of his own life.

Jeffers scourges "the jellies of arrogance and terror" of human eye and brain, and feels the human can only pollute and dilute natural beauty, order. His Calvinism seems based on hate of self, and love of seeing. He accuses God, and juxtaposes idyll and tragedy, casting himself as Cassandra in America's doomed Troy, wishing for the end to come and be over with. But he is no writer of tragedy, because he has no pity or compassion. If humans are beyond sympathy, we have only lament, not tragic figures. If man is worse than worm, there can be no tragic sense of his predicament, no catharsis through pity and fear.

I believe the power of Jeffers' poetry is partly its echo of the heavy Old English line, and its ancient Anglo-Saxon sense of doom and ruin. He has the rough-hewn energy of the scop's songs, and the unrelenting gloom of "The Wanderer" and "The Grave." The only redemption is oblivion, death, though this world and its animal spirits, wind and water, are beautiful beyond description. There is a hardness, a sweep, a sadness, to which we respond without understanding why. It is as though he has found the bone under the flesh of modern English. Jeffers thrills in archaic ways we cannot describe. His poetry takes us to prehistory, to deep structures, to the essential elements of our language, in a tone not heard much since 1066. His poetry is a rough masonry "making stone love stone" in forms to resist the elements and welter of years.

The great eye of the Pacific, the silence of stones, are his witness to "the humaneness at the heart of things," before and after the wreck of human history. He is a stoic without the stoic's acceptance. His noble hatreds and disdains are matched only by his awe of the nonhuman. And though he has a strong sense of history he has no feeling at all for what is called "destiny." His particular fate seems to be that he cannot forget society, the community, though he can forget self, or use self only for looking out at nature. In his peaceful isolation he is obsessed by wars, politics, corruptions, modern history. He has none of Thoreau's delight in personal economy, accounting, separate and individual culture. And while he has absolutely no sense of humor, he constantly reminds us, like the sage of Walden, that the landscapes and stones of America are more beautiful than the architectures of Europe.

Jeffers can speak like the Psalmist or Isaiah, or the preacher of Ecclesiastes, yet he sounds in his statements more like Schopenhauer or Hardy. He belongs to the age of the naturalists, Dreiser and Norris. His power as a poet is that he can see from the deepest perspectives of time and planet. "The stones are my people," he says, and he stands outside, the voice in the wilderness of our memory, telling us what we do not want to remember. From his lair of stone and word, he watches time and earth and stars like fountains, and speaks across the silence, "the primal and latter silences."

Insect, Bowl, Horizon

1979

Reading the prose poems of Jean Follain I am first struck by the offhand manner of each text, the lack of surface tension in the voice. Each poem seems a gathering of casual comment and detail in clusters that swarm and sift the attention. If the forms of great verse poetry can be compared to crystal structure, as they have been by Osip Mandelstam and others, then these pieces in prose should be likened to molecules that cohere in the nonorthogonal vibration of their atoms.

By escaping the insistence of the verse line, the metronome of meter and symmetry of music, Follain has discovered and exiled himself to a world of synchronic imagery. The relaxed form, fictive not musical, allows him to thread nets of correspondences without traditional lyric gestures and heroic clichés, and abets both his originality and his limitations.

Follain's genius is the unexpected humble detail. The process of these poems is not so much free association as an exploring through lit particulars for a trail curving off to the horizon. His work is charged by erotic frictions and attraction between small natural objects, insects, animals, and the things made with hands, alive in a foreground that seems always to rush back through rift or association, or path of wordplay, into space. His images shiver in Brownian motion, their dance leading off to a sky beyond the text. Words and entities thrash centrifugally, held only, and just barely, by the calm gravity of the voice.

The most disparate images always reveal some connection, like bits of a shattered mirror seizing the same sun. Sometimes the fragments all show the same lack of connection. Follain will pick an item off in some corner of time, then find another and another, each more prominent and suddenly near the voluptuous sky. Even his types and generalizations have texture and location. His critics might call him a nominalist, and be right up to a point. But where is the spirit if not in the flesh, where is the body if not with an individual? His dilemma is a crucial one of art, which must be body and spirit at once.

In the best of Follain's poems the bits of experience kindle to attention like filings. The horizon becomes a retina. The natural objects lead us to the craftsman, the human, and often toward the infinite.

One day I suddenly notice this object within my sight for ten years and which in fact I had never truly seen. Likewise men forget the knick knacks in their bedrooms, the patterns of their wallpaper, the faces on their andirons, until the day they go to the other side, as some people say. Suddenly this forgotten bowl speaks to me, imposes its presence. I'm afraid it will fall from my hands, and on the rug depicting two elephants and their howdahs nothing will be left of it but shining fragments that have to be picked up sadly. The bowl used to be washed by chattering maid-servants surrounded by clouds and vapors, framed in glints of copper and tin. The world was new. In those days many men killed. Now everything plots without them against nothingness, even in the capitals where new torture-chambers are slowly moving in. I think it over, the bowl in my hands. Whatever craftsman fashioned it perhaps kept a proud look about him, a modest glance, was perhaps alone in the world.[1]

For all the remoteness and calmness in these poems it is surprising how often the cruelty of our race surfaces in both background and foreground. The violence of man and history functions as part of the astonishing paradox of being, always threatening at the edge of the still-life, present and rearing out of the luminous fact.

There is much thickness and distance in these little texts. The most casual seems to reach so far and fast back toward space we are tempted to call it surrealism. But the real power in Follain is clearly the accuracy in the unexpected conjugations, the depth of perspective. The strangeness derives from the freshness of the seeing.

A chant goes up from every object. The craftsman enclosed in it a
bit of his body that had known love well, then carried a long illness,
if it wasn't just snuffed by old age. Chant of wood, steel, copper.

1. Jean Follain, *A World Rich in Anniversaries: Prose Poems of Jean Follain*, trans. Mary Feeney and William Matthews (Iowa City, 1979). All subsequent quotations are also from this volume.

Across the centuries you hear henchmen snicker, girls laugh with
wild voices, madwomen bleat, a baby gurgle. But the object doesn't
vanish.

Thus poem 10 begins, and goes on to describe how after many transfor-
mations of ownership, use, form, the object turns up at the end as "a frail
machine. You have to think hard to remember what it's for. You turn it
over and over in your fingers while a legendary sun sets, far away." With
one quick turn he takes us from the object, which seems to be a timepiece,
to its model in the mythic and intricate periods of a heavenly body.

The poet begins poem 11: "The fineness of things gives the universe
nobility. Behind each thing a password lies hidden." He goes on in poem
13 to make a little essay on things and their contexts, echoing Saussure
that only relationships, syntax, create meaning for entities (words). It is
the relationship between poet and language and world that gives significance. None alone suffices. In that interaction the most ordinary thing becomes "a world rich in anniversaries." The plainest things are "our favorite toys," and pebbles along the road are collected like poems, "Old as
they are."

This plant, so exceptional since its flower never lasts more than a
few hours, broke into blossom on a morning the garden's owners
weren't at home. With its speckled petals, it bends in the breeze like
so many other more common flowers. There's a terrible sweetness
to everything. A colony of armored insects, old gold, has moved
into a shaded corner. Nearby, people hurry up and down steps. A
hand stops on the rail of an oaken stairway; every minute falls. At
six in the evening, the flower will be withered, the horizon will
begin to grow pale, a group of girls will start to sing with no weakness or shame.

                                                              poem 19

There is something faintly medieval in this celebrative lament of the irony
and vitality of chance. To be alert to the actual, the unexpected, trivial,
almost missed, is poetry. The poem not only catches the fullness of the
simultaneity, but the fresh vulgarity, the excess, the waste of beauty.

For all the awe of craft, of things touched by hands, and the reaching back into synchronicity, there is a constant rediscovery of death in the quotidian trivia. Sometimes the horizon is the earth instead of the sky beyond, and the wind sweeping down saying *et in arcadia ego* causes a different shudder. In poem 21 the poet says:

> A fountain topped by a grotesque grimacing mask no longer works. "What can you do?" says a voice behind shutters. Between cobblestones, a plant has pushed out a yellow shoot that just might end up not being crushed by someone. Minuscule plants growing in the cracks of walls have the best chance of survival. Lead gutters show their blue-gray. In a courtyard hammering speaks of slow, steady work. Finally, the wind comes down from the hill where tombs stand.

When a Follain poem fails it is because the necessity of its correspondences are assumed without convincing us. In 22, for example, most of the images seem made up and at best arbitrary, not discovered and assembled in the functional and potent complexity of a molecule. Store windows light up, the gutter seems to run with red liqueur. A passerby who has never written anything except his signature "senses this bursting beauty." Here the poet seems to know too well where he is going, and cannot lose himself in the abundant heaps and detours of experience that lead to the significant detail and back to the horizon.

Alchemy has been called "the art of far and near." It is the alchemic power of evoking the distant through the immediate that I admire in Follain. In poem 23 a man is whittling in a black smock that "makes him look like he's in mourning, even in girl's clothing, in a landscape where every leaf seems in place for eternity." In one sentence he moves from the simple blade to an image of what Follain calls elsewhere "absolute time." The same poem ends with a sentence that leads back to history's violence as the ongoing context for the wonder of things and craft and language.

> On a treetrunk is a tattered auction notice officially posted during a regime to be followed by one only slightly bloodier.

Follain can also reverse the poles of his association and show the foreground in a deathlike freeze while the distance seems to pulse. He begins poem 24, "Flies die on the sticky ribbon hung from the ceiling. The rings

on the coal stove burners fit each other perfectly," and goes on to talk about
the decoration and furnishing and cleaning of the rooms, about leaning out
a window, about how children stay inside in cold weather. And ends, "You
think you see a faint tremor on the horizon." We are left a little curious
and uneasy about the sky, reminded of the very uncertain context of our
world.

In poem 25 Follain explores our great desire to live safely, all risk in
the past, "catastrophe . . . done."

> So it would be a life of happy bit players: docile dogs, cunning cats,
> beautiful housemaids, bakers, delivery boys, chimney-sweeps, cob-
> blers, punctilious jewelers. "But wouldn't a life like that be despic-
> able, even with all the spectacular sunsets it might entail?" you
> think, called back to the restlessness of days present.

The last phrase shows the care with which Mary Feeney and William Matthews have translated these parables. "Restlessness of days present" might
have been rendered in many ways, but none with just the right lack of
theatricality as "restlessness," and "days present" is not only better than
"the present" or "present days" but also carries the suggestion of presence, of being present. After so much bad translation in the past two decades, work of this quality will help us believe in the art again.

Many of the young poets discovered poetry through translations in the
1960s. In Pound's and Kenneth Rexroth's versions of the Chinese, and in
Robert Bly's and James Wright's and W. S. Merwin's adaptations of French
and Spanish and South American work, they seemed to feel a new kind of
energy available to our poetry. What can be translated most easily, of
course, is image and simile; therefore much of this work was imagistic.
More difficult to bring over into the new language is the voice of the original, with all its shadings and nuances of gesture. The poets most immediately influenced by translation found it difficult to discover and develop
voices in their own language, beyond a prose vehicle for associative energy. Part of this impoverishment of voice can be blamed on the translators
themselves. The best verse translators seem to be those such as Richard
Wilbur and John Frederick Nims who try to preserve some of the formal
authority of the sources as well as the imagery and literal sense.

Matthews and Feeney began translating Follain in the mid-1960s,

partly under the inspiration of the selection of Follain's poems in the monu-
mental Bantam anthology *Modern European Poetry*. Their choice to work
with the prose poems, probably because Merwin had already done a volume of selected verse translations from Follain, has proved to be a lucky
one. In the decade since, they have printed various translations done with
the help of Follain's widow, in magazines. But instead of rushing into print
with a volume, they kept revising their versions, adding new poems, dropping others. Their art has grown far beyond the first successes of 1968.

I should not end without mentioning Follain's use of memory as an
analogue for the imagination. Poem 27 tells the story of a hat left by a
stranger and kept for years by the family, plotting out literally Follain's
technique of interaction between memory, object, and imagination. Together they make up the theater of experience where the hat waits like part
of a costume for another drama. The hat had belonged to a young soldier.

> He left so early the birds hadn't started to sing and no one was at
> the day's work. At length such objects disappear, with a slim chance
> of surfacing in the memory of an insomniac curled tight in bed in
> some downhearted district's last hotel.

Memory is a unifying current, and this time we are led from the hat
and family back through history to the soldier and the very morning he
left, and finally by the meditating elegist to the memory of an insomniac
at a specific hotel. Instead of moving from the entity in the foreground all
the way out to the sky by some surprising route and ending there, the poet
here draws us to the wide horizon of history and then doubles back quickly
to locate all in the instant of sleepless memory in the old hotel.

Another memory poem, 29, tells the story of a mathematician at the
turn of the century who, walking through the city, absent-mindedly picks
up a birdcage from a sidewalk quay and carrys it home through the busy
streets. At first this text seems more typically surreal than most Follain
poems, but it turns out to be a parable. What better image for the absurdity
of the rationalists of our age than the mathematician with his empty, stolen,
unnoticed birdcage?

> In the future the memory of such ludicrous times will flicker. Citi-
> zens who have survived the massacres will be sitting on caned

chairs, arms crossed, before their eyes the ghost of the professor all in black, his well-brushed cutaway, the uninhabited cage in his hand.

Another important motion and contrast in these poems is that between bland official action and the erotic and personal. In the instance of poem 31 we have a stifling scene of a family at dinner. The tension in the air weighs and irritates. Suddenly the poet mentions a bronze figurine of a goddess on the mantelpiece and says: "No one notices her bare breast. The craftsman left the other one draped." The only hope in the scene is the reminder, through art, of sensual pleasure. Later one of the women at the table goes to her room and looks at herself in a mirror. "She pushes out her chest beneath a black dress the sunshine bites at." Parallel to the poet's discovery of the undraped breast on the figurine, her private appreciation of her own body seems a refuge from the deadening social world. The pleasures of eros, whether in art or otherwise, provide a path sweeping us out into new perspectives, sane and significant.

Follain's eye roves, in poem 33, over a photograph of schoolchildren posing among statues and rosebushes, and finds the faces modest and suspicious, "already cruel, the town cynic might say," and again we hear the tremors on the horizon of civilization, the revolts and massacres. He moves quickly between those who have lost their way and their recovery, between well-being and terror. It is not so much that Follain sees the cyclic nature of experience as that he sees all threads crossing at once in the same fabric. In the confusion of history, the incommunication and isolation, one finds erotic immediacy, as in poem 36, where, after stressing the alienation of all, the poet adds, "A girl has got undressed, her body trembles with a soft sensation that hurts."

Follain will use a description of a man's derby to remind us that "during riots men wearing such hats were easily killed." No matter what the detail, history and its cruelty are lurking nearby. He seems to stumble more often than not on weapons and armor. Even the insects are "armored." And in poem 5 we find, "Guns are the jewelry of men." To complete an image of spring in poem 2 he says:

Now a May beetle the color of dead leaves proceeds across the glittering breastplate at this moment—possible as all things are possible—this moment which will never return.

Insect and panoply signify in the context of history, as history can mean most perceived in local detail.

Perhaps the path of indirection and surprise which I admire most in Follain is that of poem 3, where we are taken from the site of a former battlefield and the paraphernalia of war to a woman being loved.

The landscapes they walk through unseeing measure their lives; they tell themselves night should come pretty early. They look for an inn on a former battlefield. Once the plumes of a captain's head-gear concealed an impassive insect while the scarlet-coated captain felt fear approach. On his aging mount, he would master it. Spikey grasses, lobed leaves, ivy corymbs waver in a daydream of women's faces. In the hamlet the color of burnt bread, one woman, far from death and tilting back her head, lets her milk-swollen breast be kissed in the cool half-light.

The Kingdom of Childhood

1981

> There was a door. The top part had four panes of glass in it, covered with blue glazing paper and separated by a piece of wood in the shape of a cross. The blue stood for toil and forbearance. Rich or poor, despite finicky hatreds, they were the kind who liked dedicating their daughters to blue.[1]

Thus Jean Follain begins his informal memoir of Canisy, his native village in Normandy. And he opens that door for us into the world of his childhood and poetry. For him memory is the warp to imagination's woof, and we have in this short paragraph a repetition and foreshadowing of all his poetic work. Here, as in most of his poems, prose poems, and other prose works, he begins plainly and bluntly with the facts, the door, its panes, the blue paper. But by the end of the second sentence he has woven into the description an allusion to the major sacramental image of his culture. By the third short sentence he has approached the center of that culture's ethic, symbolized by the blue. And in the epigrammatic last sentence he gathers the whole community, acknowledging its disparities of wealth, its pettiness and hatreds, into one phrase connoting attitudes toward women, sexuality, family.

Beginning anywhere at all, with the most offhand observation or description, Follain quickly arrives at essential concerns. He rarely starts with an idea, but more often seizes on a humble detail, a fact, that leads him back over the terrain into history, and then to an idea that evokes a new perspective. In this case it is the blue of the paper on the window that serves as his vehicle. But by the time we have finished the paragraph, we have thought of the different strata of society, the multitude of human eccentricities and dislikes, the chauvinism of dedicating daughters to "toil and forbearance" while perhaps dedicating sons to aggressiveness and suc-

---

1. Jean Follain, *Canisy*, trans. Louise Guiney (Durango, Colo., 1982). All subsequent quotations are also from this volume.

cess, and finally we come to rest on the word *blue*. Though we have been told what the unifying color symbolizes, the word is still suggestive and ambiguous, drawing us beyond the paper and door, through hints of depression, perhaps the puritanical or risqué, to thoughts of the sky and ultimate perspectives. This sudden sweep away from a cluttered foreground is a signature of Follain's vision, a geometry we will find again and again in his work.

Some of Follain's poetry has received a belated but devoted attention in America. Louise Guiney's version of *Canisy* cannot but enlarge his audience. Because it is precise and concrete, Follain's work can be translated, but with their unique blend of plainness and unexpected regional and archaic usages the texts present special problems. In his later years Follain was often compared with that other maestro of the *text*, Francis Ponge, but he is still the imagist of memory while Ponge is a virtuoso of rigorous syntactic comedy.

The poet has written of his childhood in *Canisy*, and in *Collège*, published posthumously in 1973 and covering his secondary school years in Saint-Lô. But his true story is the biography of his imagination, and that we find in almost every paragraph of his work. He is a poet deeply at home with the earth and village, with the small objects and creatures of this world. Yet, touching the actual almost anywhere, he is led through a doorway into the cruelty of war and history. At the same time he sees events as superimpositions in the context of ideas, both scientific and theological. His vision soars from the isolated fact to the farthest conceivable horizon. Never losing the smell and feel of the earth and its variety of inhabitants, he seems to see from several different dimensions at once. In this he is at home in his century.

Follain is an epicure in the ancient sense. His work is a new interpretation of the Atomists and Lucretius, and the core of his poetry is a wise pleasure. He may not believe in the immortality of the soul after death, but he believes in its immortality in life. It could be argued that he does not know our ultimate gift is suffering; what he knows is that celebration transforms even suffering. He is not interested in tragic poses. Through the subjectivity of memory and the objectivity of language, he teases his muse with offhand manner and matter-of-fact tone of voice until she reveals the most surprising favors.

The true poem is language itself. Brush syntax with a few details and it glows with its own unity on several horizons. How Follain loves the tiny and temporal that have no designs on him for salvation or punishment, the unnoticed things that leave him to take his chances among the sprawl and clutter. He never makes a claim for examples, but following his memory and fascination with exceptions often rises to the scope of the typic. For Follain each little corner of history implies the whole. His fascination with war and violence shows up even in *Canisy* in the frequent mention of armor and weapons. They are the bright idols of history, never absent long from his thought. Neither are the erotic and sensuous; simultaneously with the brutality and pomp of history there is always a woman uncovering her breasts for a lover, a girl looking at herself in a mirror. And the odd detail, the incongruent fact, conforms to some greater perspective, beyond what we had seen.

It would be too easy to say that Follain's foreground compares to the lucid details of classical physics and art, erotic, real; that his middle distance is usually filled with war, history, violence, pomp; and that his farthest background is the horizon suggesting void and eternity. For often he will reverse the order, and after locating in some distant statement or allusion, come soaring back to a luminous detail at our feet, finding the unity only in entity. And he will fold and superimpose his middle ground so that all ages and places are contiguous, clashing and joining eras in the theater of his language. It has been said that Follain has no evident metaphors, and while it is true that he makes few direct comparisons and statements of equivalence, the fact is that his work functions almost entirely by implied metaphor, making each text a many-variable equation. A better mathematical analogy might be the matrix, where the relationships are spread out in a deceptively simple array of interpenetration, all elements aligned in several directions.

Many critics have commented on Follain's sense of time, and he himself has referred to his interest in "absolute time." What I think he means is that beyond all the other clocks in the world, the human and historical, the geologic, astronomic, and atomic, and his own inner timing of memory, feeling, recognition, he is as skeptical as Einstein that time exists at all. What we perceive as time is, in this ultimate perspective, just a bump on timespace, a function of our limited point of view. But an awareness of this last horizon does not diminish in the least the clarity with which he sees the dust being freed from rock and flesh. At the moment of perception all will and geometries are bent in concentric embrace. If matter distorts our perception, it also dilates and glows in attention's wind. According to the quantum physicist, time flows in the direction of probability, or toward increasing entropy, because that is our expectation of it. Some feel that the direction of time was set in the first second after the Big Bang when that ultimate fusion of matter began to expand and break down into smaller elements. We might just as well see time as moving in waves or circles, or backwards, if we had developed the habit. But we live almost entirely in the ruts of linear time, measuring with the clocks of declining power. Only in a few cracks in our thought, and in the analogies of poets and sages, do we glimpse the other possibilities. Follain, in his quick plotting of new coordinates, gives us a brief sense of the other dimensions intersecting our own.

If we say that Follain is a poet of objects we are telling only a partial truth. For, though he can indeed pay such close attention to things they seem strange again, and though he makes the ordinary seem priceless, and can show the value of the smallest gesture and the vibrancy of things, I suggest that his greatest power is the ability to relate accurately very different kinds of perception. It is not just that he sees the details that no one else notices, but that he sees them in the context of unexpected worlds of thought and memory. He aspires, he has said, "to seize with a glance the closed kingdoms," and this is closer to the truth. We feel, reading him, the ultimate relatedness of everything in a royalty of access that annihilates boundaries. Each object can open like a nick in the wall that is "the mystery of the present."

Canisy is perhaps Follain's most deceptive book. It must be read first as a concise and imagistic memoir, inspired not so much by nostalgia as by wonder, at the discovery of life in a village in Normandy, and the discovery of language adequate to that experience, and the passage and nonpassage of time. In this world of phrase and image, all is seen as for the first time: the two grandfathers, schoolmaster and country notary, respectively, the snuffbox and dictionary, the Bible illustration and the stripes on the soldier's pants, the old servant Florentine. *Canisy* is deceptive because it conceals most of its art. Only on second or third reading does much of the metaphoric depth become visible. The surface is a rather relaxed and rambling collection of sketches of village life just after the turn of the century. Later we begin to see that most of the text is as carefully worked as Follain's prose poems, and that the passages often function like poems, down to the meticulously shaped sentences and timed phrasing.

It is always important to read the prose of a poet because there we can see what is left out of his poems. We have a better measure not only of the art practiced, but of the foreground and context of the work. We get to look at the pots where the poet has mixed his colors, and at the berries and oils from which the colors are cooked. The work in English that comes to mind most often as I read *Canisy* is Edwin Muir's memoir of the Orkneys, *The Story and the Fable*. As Muir's book provides a startling background and atmosphere for his mythic poems, so *Canisy* gives a surprising new reference to the mysterious world of Follain's poems. It is not so much the biographies of the poets that are important, but the advantage of seeing their gifts at work with detailed literal contexts. Neither the Orkneys nor Canisy is the true home of the poetry, but having seen those places as carried in the poet's vision, we know something more substantial about the poetry.

As the real subject of Follain's poetry is not object but context and relationship, the true subject of *Canisy* is community. Not only is the poet recreating by detail and implication the literal village he knew as a child, but he is making accessible to us the discovery of community, the community of things, creatures, people, moods, and the community of time. But most of all he is recreating the discovery of the community that is language. Our deepest kinship is with the syntax of our seeing and saying, and *Canisy* is a memoir of that love.

Because Follain's firm, clear prose goes on so matter-of-factly enumerating and remembering, the sudden shifts off into metaphoric distance seem as casual and unpretentious as the facts themselves. It is the tone of easy recall that dominates, not the images and details. And what the tone accomplishes most effectively is an atmosphere in which the affection of memory and the child's royal touch turn everything they brush into perceptual gold.

The child discovers that he has inherited a realm rich in paradox and peopled by fragile but powerful women who seem to shape children out of the darkness. It is a realm wonderful with recognition, created apparently for the awe and expectation of the young explorer, who seems to rule by merely seeing. It is a world that is possible, and rewarding. When Florentine is told of an incestuous passion, she comments: "What can you expect? It's his own." She lets the little poet scribble on her white cap with an old pencil, and sings to him. She is almost a personification of the village, mothering, practical, always surprising.

It is interesting that the poet's parents are virtually absent from *Canisy*. In this world of grandparents and servants the child has an authority and audience he cannot have with those who have the real responsibility for raising him. The parents have been forgotten, and what is recalled is what treated him like a sovereign: grandparents, furniture, "debris of insects," traffic of wagons and farm girls on the road.

The cabinet of toys, the first set of chessmen, the "wise and magnetic swallow" of a forgotten game, have been lost. But there is memory realized through language, and the world to which the adult is heir, if only he can remember it. The constant interpenetration of the literary, the historical, the ordinary, and the sublime distinguishes all Follain's work, and this is a legacy of his early years in Canisy, for this joining of earth, art, death, and the heavenly characterizes almost every page of his memoir. Canisy and his poetry not only share a common border, they overlap in great areas on his poetic map. But it is not just the objects and people that he has kept alive through his art, for the joy of paradox is as important as the delight of fact in this landscape. Indeed, few delights can be sustained outside the energy field of irony. When the hired man Lécluse tells the child it is the sea he hears inside a shell, the young poet suggests it may be just a habit, the hearing of the sea. But the hired man, like some character out of a Frost poem, assumes he means the habit the shell has acquired of sounding like the sea, "revealing his simple faith in patterns as in metamorphosis. Like the daylight just then fading to marvelous velvet, the green turning black beneath a legendary sky." The truth in the hired man's point of view is the delight in correspondences not always grammatical with science but always in accord with their own authenticity. It is the paradox, the collision between the two angles of vision, that delights the poet most.

In a world of steadily retreating boundaries, not only can the young poet see the shooting stars reflected in the peasant's bowl of soup, and the legendary sky from the evening shadows in the grass, but he suddenly recognizes that every sound and image is linked with another, each unifying the world in an interlocking series of connections. One legacy of this childhood is Follain's sense that being, all being, has an inherent nobility, beyond any political or social definition. From the seat of his early vision he saw the village simpleton who talked so slowly the others had to leave him standing in the road, "heavy as a snowman, hand still raised in explanation."

But there is no description adequate to the vividness of a girl watering plants in the evening. Only rhythm and repetition can suggest the uniqueness and dignity of the act. The little girl "starts to walk across the room, with immense care holding an overflowing bowl; she articulates her young skeleton, she is going to pass, she is passing, she has passed." This freeze-frame, slow-motion conjugation is almost commensurate with the tension of the image.

Canisy ends when its hero is ten, just before he goes away to school to prepare for his professional study and the enterprise of poetry by which he will retain the world he is leaving. The conclusion is appropriately elegiac, the close of childhood foreshadowing the end of a lifetime. The atmosphere is that of the passing of a lord, and the images, though realistic, amplify the slow, spectacular music.

The mighty edifices of nightfall: triumphal arches formed by foliage at the end of avenues, labyrinths of cool paths, fields like coliseums with hedgerows for bleachers all the way to the horizon, porticoes and dolmens of cloud framing our childhood being as it travelled towards its destiny.

The Compound Vision of A. R. Ammons' Early Poems

1973

Ommateum, A. R. Ammons' first book, was printed in 1955. The costs of publication were paid by the author, and the book soon went out of print with only one review. In *Collected Poems, 1951–1971*, it was reprinted complete except for one short poem. But the addition of four previously unpublished poems of the same period, one of them spectacularly successful, makes up for the omission. The missing poem is "Behind the I," and I will include it in my discussion, as well as the eight poems immediately following *Ommateum* that complete the first chronological division of *Collected Poems*. Since neither the volume *Ommateum* nor the early poems in general have received much critical notice, I would like to show that the major concerns of Ammons' later work are present, either explicit or implicit, in his first poems. The primary theme is the failure of the search for unity and identity. The fundamental interest is language that mirrors the multeity of experience and through which the poet seeks a unifying perception. The unity is always found in contradictions. Through language a mandala is built to image and evoke the universal sexual polarities. The paradox is arrested and fused for an instant of perception. Ammons' use of language makes the abstract and multiple immediate. With a close reading I hope to locate the preoccupations of these first elusive poems and make their excellence more accessible, as well as identify them more closely with the later work.

The word *ommateum* means "compound eye," such as an insect has. According to the foreword of the original volume, written by Ammons himself, "The poems suggest a many-sided view of reality; an adoption of tentative, provisional attitudes, replacing the partial, unified, prejudicial, and rigid."[1] Besides *many-sided*, the important word here is *provisional*. The provisional attitude characterizes these and all Ammons' poems; no

---

1. A. R. Ammons, *Ommateum* (Philadelphia, 1955).

matter how convincing and profound a discovery or point of view, he is willing to see it as tentative, valuable as an authentic point in the ongoing motion of being. We might expect a poet to attempt replacing the partial or prejudicial or rigid, but only the most far-reaching perception would from the beginning attempt to replace the "unified," rejecting what fits too neatly to look for the fragments of a more subtle unity.

The landscape of these poems is the desert, a wasteland not in the least literary but personal, chilling with emptiness and ruined distances. As the foreword says, the language is "terse and evocative." The poems have an eloquent spareness. There is no punctuation in most. They have a cutting rawness. The originality is unmistakable. Tough as scar tissue, the voice has been pared of all but the essential gestures. We have the sense of overpowering emotion contained only by language that resists the emotional. The poems are both expressions of crisis and gifts of experience. There is a wildness here, an innocence and dismay at loss.

According to the foreword (not reprinted in *Collected Poems*) the themes of *Ommateum* include "fear of the loss of identity, the appreciation of transient natural beauty, the conflict between the individual and the group, the chaotic particle in the classical field, the creation of false gods to serve real human needs." Most of the poems deal with one of these themes, some with several or all of them. The first is the subject of the first poem, "So I Said I Am Ezra."

> So I said I am Ezra
> and the wind whipped my throat
> gaming for the sounds of my voice
>   I listened to the wind
> go over my head and up into the night
> Turning to the sea I said
>   I am Ezra
> but there were no echoes from the waves
> The words were swallowed up
>   in the voice of the surf
> or leaping over the swells
> lost themselves oceanward[2]

2. A. R. Ammons, *Collected Poems, 1951–1971* (New York, 1972). All subsequent

Asserting an identity, Ezra expects it to be recognized by the wind and the flux of experience. But the universe is indifferent to his assertion. It does not return his voice or attention, but swallows his words into its own currents and surfs. Unaffirmed, his identity is drained away into the surrounding motions. Repeated, the assertion is eroded by the experience it seeks to order. There is a power here in the language hard to account for. The originality of phrasing such as "gaming for the sounds of my voice" and later in the poem, "seamists across the dunes" reinforces but does not explain the energy. It is the voice that convinces, beyond any parallelism or specific line. The beginning line has a rightness of simplicity and unpremeditated power, like the first line of a Shakespeare sonnet.

The speaker of these poems is a spiritual exile. He has awakened in the desert and, exploring, finds nothing but the shifting alien sand and his own being. He confronts the ruins and the sky. "The Sap Is Gone Out of the Trees" is a biblical lament of this exile: "The sap is gone out of the hollow straws / and the marrow out of my bones." The directness of the language startles. It has neither literary allusiveness nor the concreteness of imagist poetry, but demands to be understood completely on its own terms.

"In Strasbourg in 1349" is a narrative of outrage. It recounts the onslaught of the plague:

> Death walked on both sides of the Sea
> tasting Christian and Saracen flesh
> and took another turn about the Sea
> In a black gown and scarlet cape she went
> skipping across the Sea
> freeing ships to rear and fly in the wind
>   with their cargoes of dead
>   Vultures whipped amorous wings
> in the shadow of death
> and death was happy with them and flew swiftly
> whirling a lyrical dance on hidden feet
> Dogs ate their masters' empty hands

---

quotations are also from this volume, except for quotations from the twenty-fourth poem of *Ommateum*.

Though Ammons will rarely return to this dramatic narrative style, he handles it here with great power. The image of Death walking in a scarlet cape has a calmness that heightens the horror, as the line "Dogs ate their masters' empty hands" has the power of direct observation beyond poetic device. The second half of the poem tells how the Jews were blamed for the plague and burned as punishment, multiplying the dimensions of the tragedy. The speaker is so disgusted with human life he wishes himself to be dead.

> So I left and walked up into the air
> and sat down in a cool draft
> my face hot from watching the fire
>   When morning came
> I looked down at the ashes
> and rose and walked out of the world

Later Ammons is able to embrace the emptiness with something like celebration, or at least with the comfort of the song of failure. But here the breakdown of identity and the identification with landscape are complete. The only contact the self makes is with its own voice.

"I Broke a Sheaf of Light" contains the poet's first inkling that his rescue will come from inside him and not from the outside. The first "light" is not even found in present experience but in the memory. It seems this poem refers to an event in the speaker's youth, a personal radiance discovered and forgotten until it floats up again in the present. We are not told exactly what the personal illumination was, but its recovery allows the poet to find the radiance outside of himself, in the landscape. The poem begins:

> I broke a sheaf of light
>   from a sunbeam
> that was slipping through thunderheads
> drawing a last vintage from the hills
> O golden sheaf I said
> and throwing it on my shoulder
> brought it home to the corner

The "sheaf of light" is an image Ammons uses again in several other poems. It is the harvest of insight, the gathering of the elements of voice and understanding like the bundle of the "holy rods of civilization" the Sumerians treasured. This fascicle of the essentials of human experience is always the same, but must be discovered by each individual on his own. Our knowledge of this gathering of the pieces remains provisional and changing. The poem is an expression of this tentative unity. The line "drawing a last vintage from the hills" is especially striking in that it carries a sense of the light pulling moisture from the earth, reversing the motion of the shaft of falling light, and suggests that the light is fermenting, transforming what it touches. After breaking off the sheaf and taking it to his private corner the speaker returns to his chores on the farm.

> The cow lowed from the pasture and I answered
> yes I am late
> already the evening star
> The pigs heard me coming and squealed
> From the stables a neigh reminded me
> yes I am late having forgot
> I have been out to the sunbeam
> and broken a sheaf of gold
> > Returning to my corner
> I sat by the fire with the sheaf of light
> that shone through the night
> and was hardly gone when morning came

An ease and calmness come after the sheaf of light has been found and brought home. Despair is transformed into great feeling for the humble and familiar. First the speaker answers and feeds the animals, then returns to the corner by the fire. For Ammons, to "come home" is to come into the imagination. The ordinary is heightened by perception, to radiance. By stopping in midsentence with "already the evening star" the image is doubly evocative. In the corner by the fire the excitement burns all night. The final line means both that the sheaf's light does not go out when the sun returns and that there is little of the speaker left in the world of actuality.

"Some Months Ago" celebrates the freedom of nothingness, the release from the actual. The speaker lovingly recounts the objects of the earth to which he said farewell before leaving.

> Some months ago I went out early
> to pay
>   my last respects to earth
>   farewell earth
>   ocean farewell
> lean eucalyptus with nude gray skin
>   farewell

After the simple enumeration that includes "Hedgerows hung with web and dew / that disappear at a touch / like snail eyes" he steps "into the great open." The irony is that the gain of the open is the loss of the specific. The poem is both celebration and lament. The seer looks back with great affection to the things he has given up to reach his level of vision. This conflict of aspiration is expressed again in "Bees Stopped," through a quick cut from an overall view of a lake, where nothing living can be seen, to the seething life under a leaf. In the wide perspective all separate living things drain out of vision.

One of Ammons' finest poems, "Rack," was not included in *Ommateum*. We are lucky he decided to publish it in *Collected Poems*, because it is one of his most moving expressions of the fragmentation of the self. The quest of the poet is to find enough scattered pieces to build back a sheaf of unity.

> The pieces of my voice have been thrown
> away I said turning to the hedgerows
> and hidden ditches
> Where do the pieces of
> my voice lie scattered
> The cedarcone said you have been ground
> down into and whirled

The lines have a sweeping eloquence heightened by the gesture "I said turning" and the quick arcs of enjambment. The humble but fertile cedarcone appears often in Ammons' work. Although lowly it is complete, and tells the poet that not only is his voice fragmented, but it has been ground down into dust and blown over the earth. The incomplete sentence has the effect of an explosion; the line burns down like a fuse and bursts onto the blankness of the page.

> Tomorrow I must go look under the clumps of
> marshgrass in wet deserts
> and in dry deserts
> when the wind falls from the mountain
> inquire of the chuckwalla what he saw go by
> and what the sidewinder found
> risen in the changing sand
> I must run down all the pieces
> and build the whole silence back

The surprise is that what is being built back is "the whole silence." The voice is only audible in fragments, which the poet tries to gather back into silence. The poem itself is the expression of failure. In Ammons' poetry, we only recognize a motion by knowing its opposite. "Rack" demonstrates his assertion that "the poem must be greater than the sum of its parts." The authority is located and projected by the language as miraculously as persons are "beamed aboard" to materialize before our eyes in the science fiction show. The poem ends:

> As I look across the fields the sun
> big in my eyes I see the hills
> the great black unwasting silence and
> know I must go out beyond the hills and seek
> for I am broken over the earth—
> so little remains
> for the silent offering of my death

Now the poet must gather enough pieces to offer death in return for release from the searching. He must rebuild a silence to exchange for The Silence.

But the promise to the reader is that he will look everywhere and report his discoveries.

A unique characteristic of Ammons' poetry is his use of dialogues with mountains or wind. These dialogues have the deftness of fabliaux and the depth of parable. Through them he has recovered something lost from poetry for hundreds of years. Many of his early poems seem as if they had been found on clay tablets in the ruins of Babylon. They are songs of defeat, and the landscape of crumbling temples and scattered bones evokes an ancient authority. Several of the early poems refer directly to Sumer or Babylon. The surprise is the sense of newness and modernity. Simultaneous antiquity and freshness suggest the kind of contradiction the poems turn on. "I Went Out to the Sun," the first poem Ammons published, works through just this combination of serious fun and spare dialogue.

> I went out to the sun
> where it burned over a desert willow
> and getting under the shade of the willow
> I said
>> It's very hot in this country
> The sun said nothing so I said
>> The moon has been talking about you
> and he said
>> Well what is it this time
>
>> She says it's her own light
> He threw his flames out so far
> they almost scorched the top of the willow
>> Well I said of course I don't know
>
> The sun went on and the willow was glad

The speaker finds an arroyo and digs for water, which comes "muddy and then clear." Sitting back under his willow he makes an understatement of epic proportions.

> This land where whirlwinds
> walking at noon in tall columns of dust
>> take stately turns about the desert
>> is a very dry land

It is almost painful to see the image of the tall whirlwinds taking "stately turns" demolished by the completion of the sentence. The moon comes out later cooling the desert, and says:

> I see over the mountain
> the sun is angry
> Not able to see him I called and said
> Why are you angry with the moon
> since all at last must be lost
> to the great vacuity

The dismay and amusement are at the conflicts of experience, between parts of the self, male and female, earth and sky, when considered against the brevity of life and the decaying universe. Ammons, the parablist of the year 2000, strips human consciousness down to its essentials. His dialogues are fresh as the earliest written records, his myth science. He is both priest and skeptic of the cult, the visionary of positivism. He seeks and fears the emptiness of ultimate realization.

"Consignee" again celebrates the achievement of this nothingness. The speaker has descended from the "platform of noon"; life itself was the hanging. The middle stanza is a quick dialogue with death.

> To death, the diffuse one
> going beside me, I said,
> You have brought me out of day
> and he said
> No longer like the fields of earth
> may you go in and out

The response to this knowledge of final imprisonment outside the actual is:

> I quarreled and devised a while
> but went on
> having sensed a nice dominion in the air,
> the black so round and deep.

"The Whaleboat Struck" also honors the release of death. Freed from his body after running aground and being shot by natives ("the arrow sang to my throat"), the persona drifts away whirling in the thermals and talks with the wind, keeping up with the news of his body decaying and the bones bleaching on the shore. Going back for a look he finds only the immaculate skeleton.

> Breathing the clean air
> I picked up a rib
>   to draw figures in the sand
> till there is no roar in the ocean
> no green in the sea
> till the northwind flings no waves
> across the open sea
> I running in and out with the waves
> I singing old Devonshire airs

It may or may not be relevant that the poet's ancestors came to America from Devonshire, but a part of this great desire to be of the present by the imagination is the dream of achieving "absolute time," of getting back to the primal unity. The poem is the time machine. But the release from the limits of the present is still a death to the actual. "Turning a Moment to Say So Long" confronts the danger of getting too close to the Nothingness. Listening to "unsaid things" can be as frightening as facing the ruins and devastation of the desert. Startled by reaching the outer "boundary of mind," the speaker turns back and plunges into the "well" of the self. Much effort of modern thought has been directed toward isolating and expressing the pure, irreducible self, but sinking inward the poet finds fragments, debris, same as outside. Going down past the deepest roots he finds nothing but darkness. There is only the middle land of fragments and the need to assemble a unity. The question is, When was the whole shattered? Since the whole is silence, or nothingness, it can only have been destroyed at creation. A whole something is a contradiction. To Ammons the Creation is synonymous with the Fall. The unities we find other than silence, such as religion, art, and science, are illusions to be replaced. But each discovery is a temporary release.

"Turning" warns against the deceptiveness of experience. Here the speaker is wooed by the beauty of a lioness who apparently kills him, "her warm tongue flickering the living flutter / of . . . being" before he ever realizes her intentions. The difficulty of the poem is that we see everything through the speaker's eyes and never know whether he is ecstatic or dying, except by the context of the other poems. But either reading is chilling.

In "Dying in a Mirthful Place" the speaker finds himself near death among a crowd of feasting dancers, and turns to death saying, "I thought you knew propriety."

> so I watched the lips
> and hurried away to a hill in Arizona
> where in the soil was such a noiseless
> mirth and death
> that I lay down and placed my head
>   by a great boulder
> The next morning I was dead
>   excepting a few peripheral cells
> and the buzzards
> waiting for a savoring age to come
> sat over me in mournful conversations
> that sounded excellent to my eternal ear

Not only death is sought, but a death among the arid and empty, where the soil has a "noiseless mirth," and the only comfort is a boulder to place the head next to. By the end of the poem the speaker is already dead and celebrating with the buzzards that wait for a "savoring age to come" over his flesh. The phrase that really strikes home is the last, "eternal ear." This is what the poet has been seeking, an ear on the cosmos beyond time and form. The purpose of the poem is to evoke a sense of this eternal hearing.

"When Rahman Rides" is another imagining of being beyond form and time. The poem has a mystery no amount of reading can dispel. Rahman rides in "dead haste" across the desert, and the speaker like a dusty wind calls out to him as if Rahman is someone he has been waiting for. But Rahman, whoever or whatever he is, either does not hear or flees in fear.

> There was the rush of dust and then farther on
> a spiral whirlwinding
> as if he had stopped too late and drawing up his wings
> looked back at the saguaro's lifted arms

> Unspiralling
> he swept on across the desert
> leaving me the ocotillo in a bloomless month

It is as if separate worlds mesh but are invisible to each other. There is no enlightenment. Whatever was supposed to happen doesn't, and the speaker is left with his wraithlike existence in the desert with not even the ocotillo in bloom, and his freedom.

"With Ropes of Hemp" introduces a new image of the poet's exile and longing for release through song.

> With ropes of hemp
> I lashed my body to the great oak
> saying odes for the fiber of the oakbark
> and the oakwood saying supplications
> to the root mesh

While he chants "hysterical" to the oak and watches his body waste in its bonds,

> eternity
> greater than the ravelings of a rope
> waited with me patient in my experiment

We think immediately of crucifixion and Ulysses tied to the mast, and by now are familiar with Ammons' preoccupation with the siren call of silence and nothingness. He chants to the form, the oak fiber, that holds them. Eternity is watching his suffering. Imprisoned in the actual, he binds himself even more closely to free his voice into timelessness.

> Under the grip of my bonds
> I say Oh and melt beyond the ruthless coil
> but return again saying odes in the night
> where I stand splintered to the oak
> gathering the dissentient ghosts of my spirit
> into the oakheart
> I in the night standing saying oaksongs
> entertaining my soul to me

The oak fiber of song is the object into which the scattered ghosts are called. The bonds of language hold the gathering that serves as an eternal ear and identity.

"Doxology," the first longer poem that Ammons wrote, describes the same trajectory of realization as the other poems. Its texture is richer visually and the tone more formal than those of the other early work, but it is charged with the same paradox. The title of each part contains the syllable *dox*: "Heterodoxy with Ennui," "Orthodoxy with Achievement," and "Paradox with Variety." The three sections can be considered thesis, antithesis, and synthesis, or perhaps Christ, the Holy Spirit, and God the Father. The second half of each title refers to the human experience of that stage. Emotionally the first section expresses passion, desire for knowledge and dominance, or maleness, the second peace and sympathy, or the feminine, and the third the conflict between the two, which is unresolvable. The speaker of the first part desires to transcend destruction and move with turbulent energy.

> I have heard the silent owl near death
> sees wildly with the comprehension of fire;
> have drunk from those eyes.

Sensory experiences are "unvigiled bastardies of noise." He dreams of pouring through forms and fragments "thin and fleet."

> I die at the vernal equinox
> and disorder like a kissing bug
> quaffs my bonds:

Disorder destroys the forms he takes but also frees him. In the second part the new "orthodoxy" is silence, placidity. The speaker finds the sound of his voice "a firmamental flaw." The ideal is the perfection of nothingness.

> the drought of unforested plains,
> the trilobite's voice,
> the loquacity of an alien room troubled
> by a blowfly, requires my entertainment
> while we learn the vowels of silence.

In the final section the attempt is to resolve the two forces as expressions of each other.

> Red blood is interesting:
> its vessels on the snow
> are museums of eternity.

A broken grape upon a statue "clarifies eternity." Passion is an expression of nothingness and form is a translation of disorder. Transience is a kind of permanence. But the paradox is elusive and is no sooner found than lost. The polarities remain separate and in conflict. The poet is compelled to attempt unification.

> Sometimes the price of my content
> consumes its purchase
> and martyrs' cries, echoing my peace,
> rise sinuously like smoke
> out of my ashen soul.

The nothingness lying behind experience is the subject of "My Dice Are Crystal." The clear dice, "inlaid with gold," are the forms of being under the spell of fate, which is randomness. Like Mallarmé's cosmic dice of the Milky Way, these are the images from which we try to read meaning. The question is how to read them.

> coming to rest
> the dice spoke their hard directive
> and melting
> left gold bits on the soil

Just when they come to rest and a reading is imminent the forms dissolve, leaving only flecks of gold in the dirt. Almost at the point of revelation the surfaces vanish under attention. The god has spoken but we are no wiser. I am reminded of science, which, gathering fact after fact, finds the data contradictory, instead of pointing to a unifying principle.

Next, the poet turns to ask why he should bother with the search or labor to communicate his failures. Is anyone listening, and if so, does anyone understand? In "Having Been Interstellar" he asks whether he has failed in communication as well as in the quest for unity.

> Having been interstellar
> and in the treble clef

by great expense of
    climbing mountains
    lighting crucible fires
in the catacombs
    among the hunted
and the trapped in tiers
    seeking the distillate
    answering direct
the draft of earthless air

He realizes that if he disappears no one will be aware of his going.

    no one knew
that he had ever flown
    he was no less
    no more known
to stones he left a stone

The ingenious last line can be read at least three different ways. First, the people (stones) remain stones after his effort and going away; second, he leaves with the inscrutable objects of the world another equally inscrutable object; and third, he leaves the unchanged world unchanged himself, for all his discoveries as limited and confused as ever.

One of the most difficult of Ammons' early poems is "When I Set Fire to the Reed Patch." A fire set in a dry field, the popping and crackling, draw alerted armies who fire at each other through the blaze and fight hand to hand amid the flames. The speaker who lit the burning reeds says:

I laughed my self to death
and they
legs afire
eyelashes singed
swept in flooding up the lovely
expressions of popping light
and hissing thorns of flame

But dying among the smoking reeds the soldiers

> left deposits
> that will insure
> deep mulch for next year's shoots
> the greenest hope
> autumn ever
> left this patch of reeds.

The difficulty of the poem is in reading the final stanza. Unless the irony is understood the last lines can be taken as a celebration of the deaths that enrich the soil. Actually they are a sarcastic comment on the way people help harvest themselves. Because of the other celebrations of failure and death the poem might be easier to apprehend if read out of the context of *Ommateum*.

One of the strongest expressions of the desire to transcend comes in "I Struck a Diminished Seventh." This is the chord that is the penultimate step in a progression before resolution. Striking it the poet aches for that finality, the translation to "the Universal word."

> Come word
> I said
> azalea word
> gel precipitate
> while I
>   the primitive spindle
> binding the poles of earth and air
> give you
> with river ease
> a superior appreciation
> equalling winged belief
>   It had almost come
> I perishing for deity stood up
> drying my feet
> when the minor challenge was ignored
> and death came over sieving me

The poet offers himself as the bridge between contradicting forces through which the final articulation can pass. He is so confident after striking the diminished seventh that he stands up "perishing for deity." Getting this close to the absolute it is painful to turn back, taking the option of modulation. The challenge of his advanced progression is ignored. Death strains the challenger from the flow of life and nothing else is changed.

Increasingly in Ammons' work the voice of the poet is identified with the wind. It seeks the prevailing permanence, to be elusive, describing temporary figures of great complexity. The wind is provocative and generates music in the emptiness.

> In the wind my rescue is
> in whorls of it
>   like winged tufts of dreams
> bearing
>   through the forms of nothingness
>   the gyres and hurricane eyes
> the seed safety
>   of multiple origins
>
> I set it my task
> to gather the stones of earth
>   into one place

It is the compulsion to gather the broken pieces to a whole from which the wind saves him. The task of assembling is as futile as the tower of Babel. Wind like the imagination "sowing its dreams" has rescued him:

> and telling unknown tongues
> drawn me out beyond the land's end
>   and rising in long
>   parabolas of bliss
> borne me safety
> from all those ungathered stones

Only the "multiple origins" of mind and wind carry the "safety" beyond the maddening specific labor. Wind is the circulating energy that will not take permanent form, but fills whatever it inhabits for the moment. The poet's sympathy to this permanence through alteration is related to Keats's "negative capability." It is the suppleness that allows the imagination to survive through multiple identities and arrivals.

The permanence of the wind over the objects it erodes is seen from a different attitude in "A Treeful of Cleavage Flared Branching." The speaker, feeling himself split by diverging forces, sits down in the desert to recollect the dissociated "branches" of himself. As a symbol of his faith he heaps an "altar-cone of sand" and invests it with dreams of water and growth. Both sun and wind are anxious to claim his garden of privacy. Through worship of his small cone of meaning he hopes to realize an over-all unity. The speaker asks his self-tree to grow shade-creating leaves as a sign his private god is authentic.

> the wet cuticle of the leaf tipped in shade
> yielded belief
> to the fixed will and there
> where the wind like wisdom
> sweeps clean the lust prints of the sun
> lie my bones entombed
> with the dull mound of my god
> in bliss

The key to reading this poem is the irony of the ending. Though fixed will and final belief are death and entomb the speaker with his absolute faith, unlike the wind whose wisdom is ceaseless transformation, the speaker survives even beyond death in the bliss of his limited vision. He is the serene madman smiling inside a personal enchantment while the universe rocks and crumbles around him. We who see his bones from outside the fixed belief are terrified, and move on like nomads. In the desert it is safer to keep to the shade by day, away from the illuminating sun.

The twenty-fourth poem of *Ommateum* was dropped from *Collected Poems*. It is an ingenious play on the "I" of identity. Since the fixed center of consciousness is madness or death, how is the "I am I" realization to be located in provisional existence? Looked at too closely the self disappears, can only be seen as "another," as reflected in experience. That perceived outside the self is "whole / beyond realities / I / never wants to lose." Besides the pun of "I-beam" and "eye beam," the poem contains a buried reading of "I is / an I / elated" as "I is annihilated" and "I is an eye elated." The poem is an arresting of this many-faceted paradox. The Self cannot be seen directly, except as the Other. The gain of freedom is loss of an identity.

"I Assume the World Is Curious About Me" returns to the question of the poet's relation with the rest of society. The poem is another instance of Ammons' preoccupation with the one:many problem, its real power coming in the third stanza, where the poet's very separation from others through his searching, his alienation, is seen as an act of love, a labor serving the many. The poem ends with an image of identity.

> I assume many will crowd around me
> to praise my unwillingness to simplify
> then turning
> assist in raising me to my outstanding tree
> someday unhang my sinews from the nails
> let down the gray locust from the pine

Elevation is equated with crucifixion, and the poet after death is compared to a weathering locust nailed to a pine. The songs have a permanence like the unrotting locust, but must be held in mind by the softer, still living pine. However, unnailing the sinews and casting them to oblivion is an act of mercy.

"The Grass Miracles" reminds me of Whitman's "Beginning My Studies," but whereas Whitman's poem is a pure celebration of the elementary and common, Ammons' considers the irony that it is as easy to get lost in the concrete and elementary as in the abstract. The closer it is examined, the more complex and many-sided the simple becomes, until it is diverse beyond conception. Looking too closely at the most ordinary thing means getting lost in its multiplicity. The actual must be edited by attention; otherwise the vision gets "stalled in the deadends / of branching dreams."

> I have not been industrious this autumn
> It has seemed necessary
> to accomplish everything with a pause
>   bending to part the grass
> to what round fruit
> becoming entangled in clusters

> tying all the future up
> in variations on present miracles

The last lines are a warning that the future cannot be read as variations on present experience, however miraculous it seems. The safety and vitality are in moving on.

The difficulty of these poems is not only in the reading and interpretation, but in finding a response to the ambiguities that accurately mirror experience. "I Came in a Dark Woods Upon," "One Composing," and "A Crippled Angel" are all comic asides on the paradoxical role of the poet. The first parodies the self-conscious Freudian-mythic poem. The second puns in the first line on the phrase "seminal works." The poet who is composing seminal works says, "Time is a liquid orb / where we swim . . . pursuing among the nuclear sediment / the sweet pale flakes of old events," meaning time is a smelly cunt. But there is something half serious in all this. In later work Ammons again and again compares the poem to the sexual act, the focusing of all energy to a single point of contact between opposites. The third poem begins as a tongue-in-cheek look at the Orphic myth of the poet's energy arising from suffering. The foreword of *Ommateum* says, "Forms of thought, like physical forms, are, in so far as they resist it, susceptible to change, increasingly costly and violent." By refusing to take the myth seriously at first the listener is all the more overwhelmed by the music of the suffering and crippled angel.

> and the angel
> saying prayers for the things of time
>
> let its fingers drop and burn
> the lyric strings provoking wonder
>
> Grief sounded like an ocean rose
>   in bright clothes
> and the fire
> breaking out on the limbs rising
> caught up the branching wings
>   in a flurry of ascent
> Taking a bow I shot transfixing
> the angel midair

> all miracle hanging fire
> on rafters of the sky

Setting the whole sky afire, the angel is "transfixed midair" by the poet, caught in language and nailed down on the page.

The poet's resistance to the poetic in himself is the subject of "Dropping Eyelids Among the Aerial Ash." From his lofty vision "where the silver moon / keeled in sun was setting" he can see that the suffering below may give rise to understanding and, as with the crippled angel, produce music with "powers of mercy." But this is no help to the suffering. The speaker descends from his cloud of the sublime

> and went back down into the wounds and cries
> and held up lanterns for the white nurses
> moving quickly in the dark

"I Came upon a Plateau" is one of Ammons' bitterest expressions of destruction after the cataclysm. As the foreword says, the plateau suggests the monotony of human experience. Seeking to transcend, the speaker calls "off rings / to a council of peaks."

> I said
> Spare me man's redundancy
> and putting on bright clothes
> sat down in the flat orthodoxy

Even though he shouts and puts on the "bright clothes" of ideas, the plateau is still flat. A snake goes by drawing "thrust in sines / and circles" in the white sand. Everything is bleached. "I caved in upon eternity / saying this use is colorless." The inversion of "color is useless" to "use is colorless" recharges the language. The second half of the poem describes a "pious" person who during the holocaust went into the temple to gather "relics of holy urns."

> Behold beneath this cloak
> and I looked in
> at the dark whirls of dust
>
> The peaks coughing bouldered
> laughter shook to pieces

and the snake shed himself in ripples
across a lake of sand

This poem has a compactness of expression unusual even for Ammons. The "bouldered laughter" suggests both the mocking of the universe and its decay to pieces and dust. This is perhaps the key poem to *Ommateum*. Its bitterness is caught in the imagery. The reader is left with the enigmatic objects and motions of the desert. There are no sermons or laments. It is the final poem of the volume, and it has a finality. It burns with a permanent acid vision.

The *Ommateum* poems occur in remote points of desert and mind, which is their difficulty and purity. The later poems create a sense of space more accessible and easier to recognize. Their landscape is often the more life-promoting sea shore and marshes. Even the poems that immediately follow in *Collected Poems* have less ambiguity of phrasing and are easier to respond to. There is an almost sensual apprehension of disorder and anxiety. Still, they are ironic celebrations of the freedom found in lieu of unity. But always the motion, like the charge up a glass mountain, is toward unity.

In "Whose Timeless Reach," the use of line breaks to create double and triple levels of meaning is raised to the point of genius. The Ezra persona appears again, and life itself is described as a portage.

I Ezra the dying
portage of these deathless thoughts
stood on a hill in
the presence of the mountain
and said wisdom is
too wise for man it
is for gods and gods have little
use for it . . .

Almost every line evokes a separate image that is altered by reading the line that follows as with "wisdom is / too wise for man it / is for gods and gods have little / use for it . . ." Also, the image of the speaker standing "on a hill in / the presence of the mountain" is a perfect rendering of the poet's state of achievement, reaching the vision of the hilltop only to stand in the presence of the unreachable absolute. To arrive, but into failure. The most memorable words of the poem are the central lines: "The eternal will not lie / down on any temporal hill." This one sentence evokes the pivotal irony of the poem, and of most of Ammons' work. It expresses the two contradicting realizations that hold the poet under great tension. First, the eternal does exist; there is that certainty. Second, it does not lie in its manifestations; each is true for a specific time and place. But that separate truth will not lead you to ultimate Truth, will not even take you close to the peak of the mountain, and will not come to rest on any specific hill. The seer, having reached the hilltop from which he knows that the absolute is present, must be tantalized and defeated with the glaring peak within sight. In the second half of the poem, the mountain itself speaks, attempting to comfort the poet by offering the ease and unity of his death. But the poet, still pursuing his vision of unity-in-life, stokes his dream to an even higher pitch.

> The frozen mountain rose and broke
> its tireless lecture of repose
> and said death does
> not take it away
> ends giving halts bounty and
> Bounty I said thinking of ships
> that I might take and helm right
> out through space
> dwarfing these safe harbors and
> their values
> taking the Way in whose timeless reach
> cool thought unpunishable
> by bones eternally glides

A spare but original vocabulary, as well as the happy line breaks, is responsible for the great force of the poem. The mountain "broke / its tireless lecture of repose," and the speaker dreams he "might take and helm right / out through space." Not only does he dream of finding some ship of imagination to sail him into the eternal, but he dreams of "helming right," as he later demands of himself that he "get right," tune and align himself with the prevailing force as with the trade winds. Of course, the

Way is death, where the mind's "cool thought unpunishable / by bones eternally glides." "Whose Timeless Reach" is a lofty act of the imagination because of the great accuracy and alertness of its language. The sublime is reached only through the humble assemblage of words, which is the real Bounty ship of imagination.

"Driving Through" focuses on the pause or interruption that releases the imagination. Coming to a halt allows the attention to begin over again, making the discovery that leads to unifying celebration. Here the ritual takes place in the moonlit desert. The flat plain is a "parting lake-gift," and its shrubs are "fontal." The desert has become a wonderland, the atmosphere cool like the cosmic currents.

> The mountains running skidded
> over the icy mirages of the moon
> and fell down tumbling
>   laughing for breath
> on the cool dunes

The sand is no longer scorching and frustrating as the tobacco fields of the coastal plain. By morning the vision has passed.

> I sat down against a brimming smoketree
> to watch and morning found the
> desert reserved
> trembling at its hot and rainless task
>   Driving through
> you would never suspect
> the midnight rite or seeing my lonely house
> guess it will someday hold
> laurel and a friend

A far more difficult poem to get at is "Choice." Like many of the *Ommateum* poems, it occurs in the highly refined reaches of mind and language, and only very close attention to the latter makes it accessible at

all. But once revealed and located in the sensibility, the poem is one of
Ammons' most valuable. The poem begins:

> Idling through the mean space dozing,
> blurred by indirection, I came upon a
> stairwell and steadied a moment to
> think against the stem:

The newness of the language makes it seem all but impenetrable. Even
after we grasp that the speaker has been drifting at ground level, there is
the strange, surreal image of the stairwell, spiraling up and down around
its newel post, or "stem," like a great bean-vine. And once again arriving
at a dual threshold, the speaker hesitates, for "upward turned golden
steps / and downward dark steps entered the dark." When confronted with
the opportunity to move upward into the sublime or down below the ordinary, the failed seeker chooses to go down.

> unused to other than even ground I
> spurned the airless heights though bright
> and the rigor to lift an immaterial soul
> and sank
> sliding in a smooth rail whirl and fell
> asleep in the inundating dark
> but waking said god abhors me
> but went on down obeying at least
> the universal law of gravity:

Having failed and fallen so often back among the dust and fragments, he
avoids any attempt for the heights and, admitting that "god abhors" him,
sinks whirling down the spiral rail, "obeying at least / the universal law of
gravity." Gravity can be read in both of its meanings: emotional and
physical.

> milleniums later waking in a lightened air
> I shivered in high purity
> and still descending grappled with

> the god that
> rolls up circles of our linear
> sight in crippling disciplines
> tighter than any climb.

The shock is that descent can be the same as ascent. Hell becomes heaven, though the motion toward either is dangerous; and later in "Bridge" Ammons will find that the journey to one is the journey to the other. Both are attained by loss of the ground level, the "idling" in the ordinary, which is the real refuge from the siren call of extremity. As he falls, the speaker grapples with the force that blinds through tangled and inverted vision and has tricked him into seeking even when he tries to drift. Vision itself is perhaps the most misleading illusion of all; any order arrived at is finally a "crippling discipline" that tightens and strangles. The only safety is to be evasive and provisional as the wind.

"Interval" is written in the longest line Ammons had used up to this point, and with great variety in the line lengths and breaks, it has the sweep he will later use in "Corson's Inlet." Once again the speaker comes to an interruption, this time a stream, and halts, sitting down beneath a pine. In his dream or meditation he sees the correspondences between the shapes of the mind and the objects and variety of nature.

> and I thought God must have had Linnaeus in mind
> orders of trees correspond so well between them

The correspondence is not only between trees, but between God's mind and the trees, God's mind and Linnaeus' mind, Linnaeus' mind and the trees. In his dream here a great fiery bird lights in the high branches of the pine he sits under, and from it drops a golden feather that speaks:

> The world is bright after rain
> for rain washes death out of the land and hides it far
> beneath the soil and it returns again cleansed with life
> and so all is a circle
> and nothing is separable

Look at this noble pine from which you are
almost indistinguishable it is also sensible
    and cries out when it is felled
and so I said are trees blind and is the earth black to them
Oh if trees are blind
        I do not want to be a tree

In his dream the poet asks to be taken out of the circle between tree and man, the circulation of the elements from one form to another in time. The line "Look at this noble pine from which you are" suggests that the man is speaking from the tree itself, or is its spokesman. But to get out of the circle is to get out of time, which even death does not guarantee.

A wind rising of *one in time* blowing the feather away
forsaken I woke
and the golden bird had flown away and the sun
had moved the shadows over me so I rose and walked on

The wind rising is the conscious man in time, waking, which drives away the sun-bird, and the speaker is left in shade. But the wonder is that he can break out of the circle enough to know there is something beyond it. And even though he fails back into time, the dream has been a release and a renewal of the temporal and ordinary. The interruption over, he walks on. From his dream of the illuminating feather (pen, insight, holy bundle of rods of civilization) he awakens and moves on among the disorder with only the memory, having come close to the tonic final chord and almost understood.

"This Black Rich Country" is a celebration of the same motion. It is the resistance to the desire for unity and order that helps generate the great tension and energy of this poem. Here is the skeptic celebrating his freedom to fail.

Dispossess me of belief:
between life and me obtrude
no symbolic forms:

> grant me no mission: let my
> mystical talents be beasts
> in dark trees: thin the wire
>
> I limp in space, melt it
> with quick heat, let me walk
> or fall alone: fail
>
> me in all comforts:
> hide renown behind the tomb:
> withdraw beyond all reach of faith:
>
> leave me this black rich country,
> uncertainty, labor, fear: do not
> steal the rewards of my mortality.

It is a song of courage, a rallying hymn of the agnostic. The poem works literally and ironically. This paradox is fixed most completely by the final clause, "do not / steal the rewards of my mortality." The last line, seen separately, contradicts the sentence, asking for destruction of mortality even as it demands the uncertainty and labor of the actual.

The poem that follows, "Look for My White Self," extends the same paradox. It is both a celebration of death and a bitter lament for the loss of mortality.

> Find me diffuse, leached colorless,
> gray as an inner image with no clothes
> along the shallows of windrows: find
>
> me wasted by hills,
> conversion mountain blue in sight
> offering its ritual cone of white:
>
> over the plain I came long years,
> drawn by gaze: flat land with
> some broken stems, no gullies,
>
> sky matched square inch with
> land in staying interchange: found
>
> confusing hills, disconcerting names

and routes, differences locked
in seamless unities:

so look for my white self, age clear,
time cleaned: there is the mountain:
even now my blue

ghost may be
singing on that height of snow.

The spirit has been harvested from the actual and sings to those who may
find the body failed among the fragments, with the glaring peak in sight.
The body and self have been leached colorless as the landscape, which
mirrors inch for inch the empty sky. Even the unities found were "seamless," both impenetrable and without distinguishing features. The reader
is warned that even if he finds the wasted body, the spirit has been released
by ultimate failure to the blinding ritual cone it sought. It is the ghost the
reader should look for beyond and behind the words.

Still, the assemblage of words is necessary to locate and present the
spirit's song. The poem is a kind of lattice with which the spirit is trapped
long enough to be perceived. The final poem of this early period is an
explanation of the other poems: "Apologia pro Vita Sua." The poet's work
is again seen as the gathering of stones into a pile, the increase of which
extends the poet's range and vision, "the cairn's height / lengthening my
radial reach."

during the night the wind falling
turned earthward its lofty freedom and speed
and the sharp blistering sound muffled
toward dawn and the blanket was
drawn up over a breathless face:

even so you can see in full dawn
the ground there lifts
a foreign thing desertless in origin.

It is fitting that the wind, in its "rescue" of the poet, the force of inspiration, is also the destroyer that finally takes away his breath. The cairn left

on the desert has come from another world. It is the monument left in the sand pointing deep into the center of space and silence to which the spirit has been released, and acting as a guide and promise to whoever finds and reads its fiction.

In Ammons' work each facet of experience gives a promise of this permanence. Wind is the vernacular manifestation of the openness. The poem is the registering of the invisible presence, the otherwise unknowable current. Ten years after the end of this first period Ammons wrote the lyric called "Project."

> My subject's
> still the wind still
> difficult to
> present
> being invisible:
> nevertheless should I
> presume it not
> I'd be compelled
> to say
> how the honeysuckle bushlimbs
> wave themselves:
> difficult
> beyond presumption

The Toy-Maker's Closet

1979

I suspect Russell Edson has had somewhat less than he deserves from the critics because they don't know where to place him. He seems to bear little resemblance to the optimistic associative work of the poets he publishes with. The fact that others such as Robert Bly and Charles Simic write prose poems gives them little kinship with his stark narrative minimalism. His spareness can in no way be linked with the bland prosiness we usually find presented as prose poems in magazines. Edson might be described as a miniature Nabokov except that he avoids the surface of erudite wordplay which that late master loved. But they share an acid-rinsed vision of the human situation, a fascination with family and incest and the grotesque. Edson lacks the interest in image and detail of Nabokov, and in fact his lean style could not carry so much information. To future generations it will be clear that they belong to the same era, and felt similar terrors and displacements and exhilarations, though the scope of the Russian's knowledge and gifts gave him an expansive appreciation, whereas Edson's joy is an intense toy world, enclosed, shrinking.

The trademark of Edson's genius is often an obscenely cruel act or relationship. And the most obvious weakness of his poems is the predictability of the outrageousness once we are familiar with the formula. But in that he is like any other comic writer. Edson is at his best when read in fairly short stretches. His books should be taken in sections of ten or fifteen prose poems at once. This is not to say that his work does not accumulate into a larger vision than the single flashes of hilarity and horror that are his best writings.

Edson has both an elegance and a clarity. There is no confusion of intention. He does not pretend to be sublime or wise or autobiographical and at the same time parody all those things. But underneath the laughter we come to feel a terror of world and flesh that operates as a kind of imaginative heat and will in a sterile, rootless, suburban and urban world. The fear, and the comedy that controls it, are as truly the poetry of our suburbs as William Carlos Williams' realism. The religious implications of Edson's fables are inescapable. He tells his little fictions in an ambience of mockery, frustration, and cruelty, unredeemed except by wit.

Yet Edson has also been a poet of things. His texts are filled with chairs, vegetables, walls, that act like people, that become people. In "Because Things Get Sad, Father," from *The Very Thing That Happens,* a family tires of its house and goes into a forest because the house is getting smaller.

> No, no, screams father, I do not want my chair to get smaller. Why must things get smaller when you leave them?
>
> Because they get sad, father, said mother.
>
> I must go home and tell the house a joke so it won't be sad, screams father.
>
> No no, father, we have grown tired of our place and have gone to some other place, screamed mother.
>
> But the house is now very small and all our things are being squeezed to death by sadness, moaned father.
>
> Well I say, said mother, it's a good thing we left before we were crushed.[1]

Later, unable to make up its mind where to go, the family returns to its house anyway, "growing smaller all the while until reaching their house they had grown just small enough to fit into their tiny house." A reader not familiar with Edson's work would translate this poem as a fable about trying to break out of limitations and grow in the world, then having to give up for lack of will and imagination. I would guess that the house is best understood as a dream-closet or playhouse, and when the family gives up its pretensions to being adult they shrink back to child-size and fit again their proper home. The Aesopic moral seems to be that only when people resign their posturing of progress and maturity can they refind their true marriages with things, chair and house and dream.

Many of the poems of *The Very Thing That Happens* parody the language of prayer and service. In "We Shall Be as Worms" a father and

1. Russell Edson, *The Very Thing That Happens* (Norfolk, Conn., 1964).

mother discuss the marriage of a "worm girl" to a "worm man" and the worms' androgyny. With hilarious pomposity the dialogue celebrates new possibilities of coupling, and the new "angle of view" in death, and ends with the pseudobiblical line "We shall be as worms."

Edson never tires of inventing new combinations and situations for the things of everyday. On one page a man says: "I think that in the centre of the universe is a jelly sandwich. . . . Strawberry. . . . It's mine screamed the man's mother." On the next page there is praise for a "baked cookbook." Like his near namesake Thomas Alva, Edson is a tinkerer, an inventor in miniature, or, to use his own phrase, "a toy-maker." Infinitely repelled by the world of adults and high seriousness, he is fascinated not only with childhood and the childish, but with old age, or second childhood. As the Greeks treated all their gods as vain and fallible humans, Edson treats all his men and women, mothers and fathers, as children. They scream and shriek and kick. Reality itself is a cruel and incomprehensibly frustrating parent to be outwitted. And the satire is not always limited to the human. In "A Horse at the Window" the narrator suggests praying to horse turds just to be on the safe side. In "Dark Friends" it is the friendly flies that are celebrated.

Edson seems to see any detail, phrase, or object as material for scenarios, as little characters for a toy theater. He is addicted to the punchline and the delayed punchline. He looks to any cliché or stereotype for the possibilities of absurd theatricality. In his writings history is histrionic. For all the sense of improvisation, though, the prose poems seem to find an inevitable shape, always moving toward the outrageous. In "Ancestral Mousetrap" he describes our inheritances, cultural and psychic, as a mousetrap. "We must not jar it, or our ancestor's gesture and pressure are lost, as the trap springs shut." The trap is kept in a jewel box, with the honor due our tensions and inhibitions and failures, guilt's jewels and jewelry, signs of a covenant with pain. In "Blank Book," "all the words have fallen out" and the people are confused. Having been the mere puppets of words (the Word?), they are lost now that the book is blank. But Edson loves dolls and marionettes as much as Rilke, and fills the blankness with his own words, with stories for enactment in the abandoned space. The idea of people as sexual dolls occurs in "The Broken Daughter," from *The Clam Theater* (1973).

His daughter had broken. He took her to be repaired . . . If you'll just pump-up her backside, and rewire her hair . . .

This girl needs a whole new set of valves, and look at all those collision marks around her face, said the mechanic.

I just want her fixed-up enough to use around the house; for longer trips I have my wife.[2]

In much of his work Edson has an obsession with cycles and wheels. A man in "The Very Thing That Happens" takes a wheel as lover. The childless couple of "Infanticide" adopts a wheel. And in "The Movement" the wheel is the idea that works, the beast of burden. At other times the wheel is totemic, a sign of the cruel cycles. Adults kill children and, dead, the children become adults in "The Changeling." A baby throws up its brain in "Colic" as though trying to keep from becoming mature and "dead." The man baby of "The Cradle" is kept in the cradle all his life by his grandmother. In several prose poems there are Blakean marriages between old women and infant boys. In "The Making of an Old Maid" a baby feeds its mother "from one of the dots on its chest." If the circle from youth to age and back is vicious, at least it must contain the playful quadrant of childhood.

Perhaps the best of all Edson's doll poems is "Pinocchio's Bride," from *The Clam Theater.*

The little girl is given one of those marionettes, the kind that eventually attach their strings to people, the kind that make little girls into marionette-wives of Pinocchio.

The marionette wears make-believe clothes over his imitation body; a shirt and tie dickey, a toy jacket with toy trousers.

The little girl undresses the marionette because she is not allowed to undress her parents.

She removes the marionette's trousers to check its backside for *duty.*

The marionette smiles cunningly as the little girl enmeshes herself in wickedness.

And now, the little nub of cotton-stuffed cloth at the marionette's

2. Russell Edson, *The Clam Theater* (Middletown, Conn., 1973).

crotch, swells and bursts, and a red stick, like a Pinocchio nose, points out.

Of the three books I have read, *The Intuitive Journey* is by far the longest. Besides almost a hundred pages of new work, it includes *The Childhood of an Equestrian* (1973), Edson's longest and best single volume, in which he realizes most fully the possibilities of his form; for all the consistency of shape and quality there is the most variety of idea and character. A few texts such as "Ballast" seem merely silly, but they are very few. Most of his lean dramas spread wide reverberations of laughter and symbolic energy.

It is in *The Childhood of an Equestrian* that Edson's fascination with fatness, especially fat women, comes into full play. Fatness in his poems seems almost a spiritual state, a bigger-than-life mode of being, a grossness that scares children and makes everyone look in horror, a campy worship of goddess-sized flesh. Baudelaire in a famous poem dreams of sliding down the breasts of a giantess and sleeping in their shadow. The bride of Edson's "dream man" is "a fat woman who disguised herself as a fat woman."

> Why? sighed her mother.
> Because people will think it's a skinny woman disguised as a fat woman.
> What's the good? sighed her mother.
> Then a man'll marry me, because many men like a skinny woman quite well.
> Then what? sighed her mother.
> Then I'll take off the disguise, and he'll see that under the fat woman is another fat woman.
> And he'll think I'm an onion and not a woman.
> He'll think he's married an onion (which is another disguise), said the fat woman.
> Then what? sighed her mother.
> He'll say, oh what a kick, an onion with a cunt.[3]

The title poem of *The Childhood of an Equestrian* is an allegory about a child falling off his horse and meeting a nursemaid in the forest. Both

3. Russell Edson, *The Intuitive Journey* (New York, 1976).

imagery and storytelling are reminiscent of Blake's "The Mental Traveller" and "The Crystal Cabinet." Edson's poem is written in the form of a dialogue, and through repetition and variation he builds a dreamlike, hypnotic atmosphere. While parodying Blake and Wordsworth as well as Freud, the poet weaves a thick texture of his own.

> The child that falls from his rockinghorse refusing to remount fathers the man with no woman taken in his arms, said the nursemaid, for women are as horses, and it is the rockinghorse that teaches the man the way of love.

But the "equestrian" has already fallen from his horse, presumably by being born, and when the nursemaid offers, "Let me help you to your manhood," he rejects her, hoping to avoid the confused circles of the metaphor. He wants to bypass the conjugations and become an "equestrian" on his own. "I lift all that fall and are made children by their falling," she says. That is precisely what he fears, "falling" into her, becoming as a little child between her legs to refind his manhood. He beats and thrashes "the fleeting white shape that seemed like a soft moon entrapped in the branches of the forest." The last images suggest not only the elusiveness of her nature to him, but also that she is trapped herself in *the same* forest, whether she pleads or leads or flees.

Because of the humor Edson is free to pursue his fancy in ways few dare in these post-Freudian times. His poetry should not work, but more often than not it does. His strengths are not only irreverence and surprise, but knowledge—in particular, knowledge of what he fears and delights in. In the belch and fart poems of *The Childhood of an Equestrian,* we are in the presence of an adult child still terrified of the grown-up world. The man and woman in "The Distressed Moth" lecture a moth on the impropriety of eating her hair and then belching. They end up quarreling about how to instruct the moth.

> But you also farted, said mother.
> Oh that was just a little aside which I thought you hadn't heard, sighed father.
> The moth farted.
> Now see what you've done! screamed father.

In these poems there are frog lovers, frog children, sex with cows, comedy in the thinness and quickness of it all. Edson is fascinated by the sex of the very old, for their androgyny as much as the grotesqueness. He reverses the direction of the Blakean conflict in "The Pattern."

A woman had given birth to an old man.

He cried to have again been caught in the pattern.

Oh well, he sighed as he took her breast to his mouth.

The woman is happy to have her baby, even if it is old.

Probably it had got mislaid in the baby place, and when they found it and saw that it was a little too ripe, they said, well, it is good enough for this woman who is almost deserving of nothing.

She wonders if she is the only mother with a baby old enough to be her father.

One of the best poems of *The Childhood of an Equestrian* is called "The Toy-Maker." In many ways it describes the maker of these poems and his love of tiny perfections and the dirty punchline.

A toy-maker made a toy wife and a toy child. He made a toy house and some toy years.

He made a getting-old toy, and he made a dying toy.

The toy-maker made a toy heaven and a toy god.

But, best of all, he liked making toy shit.

Edson's more recent work in *The Intuitive Journey* and *The Reason Why the Closet-Man Is Never Sad* is not as consistently excellent as *The Childhood of an Equestrian,* but he introduces several new variations of the prose poem, and the best of this work is among his strongest. All the familiar themes are there: the domineering mother who is almost Edson's muse, the marriage-war poems with their ritual cruelties, the apes and mice and toys. And yet it should be said that there is no sense of growth in these later books. While the level of accomplishment is high, one feels that Edson may have reached the potential of his art in *The Childhood of an Equestrian.* It is possible that the limits inherent in what he does, in the attitudes and obsessions and rejections that make his work so haunting, have been found. His particular kind of sympathy and lack of scope keep him to this one music. Apparently Edson is aware of this, and in "The Prose Poem in America" in *Parnassus* he surveys recent work in the form and then compares the possibilities of the prose poem to those of verse poetry.

> Poetry is inherently joyous, no matter how gloomy its seeming content sometimes; this is because time does not destroy its energy as it does with prose; prose is always running out through time. Poetry, by its very psychology, celebrates everything it touches; its psychology is based on the idea of eternal life.
>
> It is the bringing together of poetry's sense of continuous life, and the darkness of prose, that makes the prose poem unstable, intelligent but always remaining, no matter how well made, an unfinished form. Gladness and the sense of dread so combined is [*sic*] very often to be answered only by laughter. In my view, the basic contradiction from which the prose poem springs is a comic understanding. For in the prose poem one feels *the all too real* coupled with the artificial sense of art aware of itself.[4]

As an "unstable form" the prose poem is the product of a transitional period in American poetry, a way of keeping the imagination at work and searching for a new beginning. For all of its limitations the form seems to answer a need of our times. Edson concludes: "Let's work in an unstable form for a while. When poetry is ready to sing again it will."

The prose poem still seems a relatively recent invention to most of us. That prose *poetry* is old as Melville, old as Ossian, old as the Old Testament, is widely accepted. But the idea of the prose *poem* is more suspect, considered an import from France, or worse, the product of the upstart young who do not want to trouble themselves with the proper job of writing verse.

There is some ground for these suspicions. Obviously the poem in prose will not have the crystalline perfection of form of the best verse, nor the memorability of rhymed and regular lines, nor will it have the happy increment of energy that the line break gives. It has been understood that Baudelaire and many French poets of the nineteenth century developed the

4. Russell Edson, "The Prose Poem in America," *Parnassus: Poetry in Review* (Fall/Winter, 1976), 321–25.

poème en prose to escape the alexandrine and all the built-in conventions and limits of French versification. But in contemporary American poetry, where most of the work is being written in very free verse probably too near prose already, what advantage is there in going all the way and practicing "the prose poem"?

A few years ago I looked through a thick paperback anthology called *The Prose Poem*. The selections from other countries and languages seemed to include interesting texts, but the section of American writing looked surprisingly unimaginative, as if to justify our skepticism about prose poems, at least for writers working in English. Suddenly I came on the selection of Edson's poems and realized I was in the presence of a gifted storyteller. All the worry about prose versus poetry, line versus sentence rhythm, vanished. The telling of the miniature dramas was compact and crisp, the narrative always compelling and, even at its most absurd and silly, refreshing, as one scenario and character after another lived for a few seconds on the frame of the page and in the mental theater.

Later I came on Edson's piece in *Field*, "Portrait of the Writer as a Fat Man: Some Subjective Ideas or Notions on the Care and Feeding of Prose Poems." Beginning with a fable about the poet as fat man sitting down to write about a fat man sitting down to write, Edson moves on to a considered and sophisticated discussion of his medium. The critical speculations are woven into an allegorical drama of himself writing them. His ideas about writing all turn into little stories: "All is will and power, both growing from the other like a single club, with which I shall force a fiction—as though I scrubbed floors to send my son through college that he might get a high-paying job and buy me a castle to live in, where I spend my remaining days simpering and whimpering about how I went down on my knees with a scrub-pail to send my son through college."[5] After the Fat Man spins out several stories of the writer as scavenger and microbe, as tormentor and glutton, he becomes skeptical of the whole enterprise of writing a novel about a fat man writing a novel, about writing about writing, and of the bigness of the novel, and says: "It was as if to buy a farm you bought a cabbage. The fat man smiled and fell out of his head."

Edson, or the Fat Man, is scared of his speculations, and by the twen-

5. Russell Edson, "Portrait of the Writer as a Fat Man: Some Suggestive Ideas or Notions on the Care and Feeding of Prose Poems," *Field*, No. 13 (1975), 19–28.

tieth century, and the alienation of human intelligence from the "mindless-
ness" and "endlessness" of cosmological process. He is not going to be a
poet celebrating nature. Frightened by fatal and vast redundancies, he will
cherish wit and artifice. Part of the thrill and terror of this making is its
complete isolation from the natural universe and history, especially literary
history. The Fat Man, or prose poet, "must work toward bits and pieces
formed from memory. . . . And yet experience remains hidden and less
important than the inscape it has formed. To find a prose free of the self-
consciousness of poetry; a prose more compact than the storyteller's; a
prose removed from the formalities of *literature*." One of the illusions of
the poet working in the isolation of his originality is that what he is doing
is not considered *literature*. For most American writers this has been a
transforming fiction, an enabling idea. Only by turning away from the idea
of English and European literature could Emerson, Whitman, and Twain
create their own. In this way Edson is true to the mold of the great American eccentrics, and though he may see through the paradox at times, it is
one he feels and follows. The Fat Man continues: "We are not interested
in the usual definitions, for we have neither the scholarship nor the ear. We
want to write free of debt or obligation to literary form or idea; free even
from ourselves, free from our own expectations. . . . There is more truth
in the act of writing than in what is written."

For all the air of avant-gardism and surrealism and dada in Edson's
work and theory, it is startling how closely he fits the paradigm of the
American recluse. Like Dickinson and Thoreau and perhaps Wallace Stevens, Edson seems to communicate best from isolation, to be most ecstatic
in a heretic's alienation. He is the most recent of a long line of those
who sought the privacy of attic or wilderness to pray, meditate, or give a
full and true accounting of their mental warfare. For all the surface of
arty experimentation, Edson as artist is closer to that often-blasphemic
imagination than he admits. "Your own garden, your own meditation—
isolation!—Painful, necessary!" Attacking all institutions, creative writing programs, literature, he continues: "The trouble with most who would
write poetry is that they are unwilling to throw their lives away. . . . They
are unwilling. . . . How I hate little constipated lines that are afraid to be
anything but correct, without an ounce of humor, that gaiety that death
teaches!"

The Fat Man objects most to "the self-serious poet with a terrible sense of mission," without humor or playfulness, without inner health but showing public anger and self-righteousness. He says, "Beware of serious people, for their reality is flat." Also he dislikes the "I" poem, without dramatic otherness and possibilities, without humor. Yet one arrives at this freedom to play from the place of desperation, or as the Fat Man says, "Writing is the joy when all other joys have failed." The prose poem is the little more that is left when everything else is gone. Decay and death and emptiness free the Fat Man to create funniness and silliness; "the Angel of Joy prescribes it."

Thus, the essence of the prose poem is its humor. Instead of polish, regularity, "beauty," the prose poem has its "dimensional quality" in humor. Because it is the place to forget all talk of form, and think "only of content," the prose poem takes poetry back to story and character. Of course that release brings the writing toward form again, but the transforming rejection is necessary. "Let those who play tennis play their tennis," Edson says, answering Frost, and in an especially telling sentence adds that the prose poem should look "somewhat like a page from a child's primer, indented paragraph beginnings, justified margins." To convince us of his irreverence Edson even says he is proud of the prose poem's "clumsiness, its lack of expectation and ambition," sounding almost Whitmanic in his insistence. "Any way of writing that isolates the writer from worldly acceptance offers the greatest creative efficiency. Isolation from other writers, and isolation from easy publishing. This gives one the terrible privacy so hard to bear, but necessary to get past the idea one has of oneself in relation to the world." The making in intense isolation translates into an understanding universal, joyful. No theory could be more essentially ascetic, more rebelliously puritan.

The prose poem is an approach, but certainly not a form; it is art, but more general than most of the other arts. This may sound odd because we know prose poems as things written on paper . . . the spirit or approach which is represented in the prose poem is not specifically literary. . . . If the finished prose poem is considered a piece of literature, this is quite incidental to the writing. This kind of creating should have as much ambition as a dream, which I as-

sume most of us look upon, meaning our nightly dreams, as throw-
away creations, not things to be collected in a book of poems.

The modesty or ambition of Edson's claims for his prose poems may or
may not be entirely tongue-in-cheek, but the value of this antiliterary attitude for him as active writer cannot be doubted. His very rejection of the
perfected verbal object as a goal allows him the recklessness and energy to
achieve it, in much the same way that Stevens' early discovery of and
preference for *poésie pure* enabled him to become rather quickly a great
philosophical poet.

In "The Double Bed," from *The Reason Why the Closet-Man Is Never Sad*,
Edson returns with glee to his motif of the unmarried and unmarriable
daughter. The problem here, as might be expected, is fatness; the daughter
has been "turning into a double bed." Her parents fuss over her and worry
what kind of bed she is turning into. The doubleness of the bed suggests
not only bisexuality but a sexual completeness or autosexuality.

> . . . O, yes, it helps when you're married, it's such a lonely thing
> for a woman to become a double bed all by herself, murmurs her
> mother in the dark.
>
> The woman thinks, it's a lot more comfortable, even in a double
> bed, to be alone.
>
> And she lies alone in her double bed, the double bed she has
> become, staring up at the ceiling in the dark . . .[6]

One of Edson's finest poems of family cannibalism is "Erasing Amy-
loo" in the same volume, in which a "father with a huge eraser erases his
daughter." In the kind of repression that allows us to forget the rape and
plunder of family warfare, the man and his wife erase their daughter and
rub out all memory of her, and of each other. The family cruelty can be
backward- as well as forward-looking, as in the reverse generations of "The
Parental Decision," where a man splits to become an old man and an old
woman.

6. Russell Edson, *The Reason Why the Closet-Man Is Never Sad* (Middletown, Conn.,
1977).

They must be his parents. But where is the man? Perhaps he gave
his life for them . . .

I ask the old couple if they've seen their son.

The old woman says, we've decided not to have any children.

Among the new poems in *The Reason Why the Closet-Man Is Never
Sad* is "The Rich Nearsighted Man," whose subject has all his windows
ground to his prescription. "The Long Picnic" seems at first more "poeti-
cally charming" than we expect of Edson, but the poem turns out to be a
parody of nostalgic elegy and awe for the Word. "An official document
blows through a forest between trees and over the heads of picnickers." It
is the end of summer, the food is going bad, a young man's girlfriend is
suddenly old. They cannot catch the blowing document, but the message
on it is, "*the summer is over.*"

The closet of the title poem is in fact the enclosed world of Edson's
imagination. It contains the secret and deviant self, the world of daydreams, introversions, alienation, private delight. The closet is the poet's
surreal garden where he nurses complex sexual dramas. The isolation and
preciousness of that space give just the doubleness wanted. The answer
suggested in the title is never given as such, but is implied.

Why do you have such a strange house?

I am the closet-man, I am either going or coming, and I am
never sad.

But why do you have such a strange house?

Because I am never sad . . .

Of course the last line can be read as partly sarcastic. But the poem suggests that the very eccentricity of the closet, its "strangeness," is what
makes it work. The everyday "outside" world would be sad. However,
Edson does not describe a pleasure dome. The home of his dreamlife is
humble, a place for laundry and junk, with pejorative connotations. Neither lofty nor profound, it is the place where the skeletons are hung, where
the old clothes are heaped. The closet appears again in "Summer, Forty
Years Later," in which the hero "struggles out of a closet where his mother
hung him forty years ago." After all the waiting, all the patience, the closet

dweller emerges on his own and finds the sky "darker than he remembered," and the lawn and the trees also "darker." The color is gone from everything. "That little boy who is always passing the house with his wagon has turned into a little old man collecting garbage." Having finally achieved the outer, "real" world, our hero finds it less than memory and imagination in his closet, aging and disappointing.

In *The Clam Theater* Edson published a poem called "The Pleasure of Old Age," describing how "When you get old you come apart." An old woman tries to sew an old man back together, but the parts keep falling off.

> She sews your penis and scrotum on, but the thread breaks through the flesh. It just won't come right, she says.
> Still, you enjoy her fussing with your penis.

Edson returns to the sex of the old in several of the more recent poems in *The Reason Why the Closet-Man Is Never Sad,* including "The Rooming House Dinner." Here a hostess serves "shoes for dinner with a side order of stockings and girdles" to an old man.

> She is serving underwear smothered in sweat and lack of bathing, slipping off her backside in an old rooming house where someone knows the back way to her vagina—loves it that way! He is such an animal!
>
> Oh, how she rolls her stockings into doughnuts on her ankles!
>
> The old man wants her breasts: where are they, where are they?! On my chest, where else?
>
> Yes, yes, of course. And so he has sex between her breasts.
>
> He is rolling in her underwear, asking where she keeps her mouth—her rectum!—Wants one of the doughnuts on her ankles with coffee in her shoe!
>
> He wipes his mouth and says, it's one of the best rooming house dinners he's ever had . . .

For all the laughing at the old and fat in these poems, there is something humanizing in their familiarity also. How many contemporary poets can talk about the sexuality of the old, especially with humor? Without the laughter it would not work.

Unlike most American poets, who rapidly decline in their forties after becoming a little celebrated, Edson shows no signs of weakening artistry. I suspect that his reclusiveness has stood him in good stead, along with the apparent modesty he brings to his enterprise and his lack of surface "seriousness." So far no one has taken him for a bard or prophet, nor canonized him. He is free to go his own strange way.

My guess is that none of Edson's later books represent any chronological ordering, but are gatherings by shape and theme from an enormous reservoir accumulated over the years. The same images appear and reappear. The monkey in "The Monkey Beaters," from *The Intuitive Journey,* is described as a person "with merely a bad case of hair." An old woman in "Hands" from the same volume buys an ape's hand for supper, but instead of eating it she watches it twitch. Edson combines his interest in elderly sexuality with his ape fetish in "A New Life," also in *The Intuitive Journey,* an idyll about an old man who dresses up as a gorilla and marries a young female gorilla in the forest. "What foresight of the costume-maker to have sewn in a bladder of gorilla sperm in his gorilla pants." As the old man-gorilla goes dancing and singing under the moon, Edson implies again that make-up and make-believe are as good as the thing itself, probably better, and certainly preferable to a sexless old age.

There are several poems about fatness in *The Intuitive Journey,* including "The Feet of the Fat Man," whose subject is "so fat his head suddenly slips down into his neck. His face looks up out of his neck. He says, what do you think, do you think I'm overdoing it?" At the end he is "only a couple of feet all swollen out of shape." Edson has refined the grossness of his fat poems to a brilliant revulsion. The indulgence, carnality, babyness, have developed into a cult. In "Another Appointment" from that volume the fiancé Alfredo is sat on by his bride and crushed.

But Alfredo, why are you dead. We're supposed to get married today.
The dead Alfredo, drifting somewhere near his body, would like to tell her that even had he lived it would've been quite impossible today because, unfortunately, he had another appointment . . .

> But already Alfredo is becoming part of the music that he hears,
> and is already forgetting what it is he would like to tell her . . .
> drifting through the window into the music of himself . . .

Always beyond the flesh and its cruelties and grossness there is the self and its dreamlife, the closet. Edson exults in the confusion of sexual identity. He is obsessed with mistaken sexual roles. The main character of "The Fisherman," who is bearded and smoking a pipe, claims to have been a woman once, and to prove it pulls a baby out of his pea jacket and begins to nurse it. People and things melt into other people and other things, get stuck, disappear, in endless metamorphosis. The persona in "Old Woman" keeps another old woman as a pet chained to a tree in her backyard. Boundaries and identities slip and drain unpredictably into each other. Distinctions are illusions of time and place.

Perhaps the best poems of *The Intuitive Journey* are the newer doll poems. "When the God Returns" has a Raggedy Ann taking over, becoming a mother figure, only to prove as cruel and dominating as the human original. Dolls and mannequins and dummies in power are no different. The evil is in the roles of power and adult responsibility. Sometimes the horror of manipulation rises to the pitch of pseudoepiphany. A pianist in "The Marionettes of Distant Masters" dreams he is hired to wreck a piano, but distracted by the beauty of a butterfly, he cannot act. Another butterfly arrives to torment the first. The pianist has a vision.

> And this is happening in his window box. The Cosmic Plan:
> Distant Masters manipulating minor Masters who, in turn, are ma-
> nipulating tiny Butterfly-Masters who, in turn, are manipulating
> him . . . A universe webbed with strings!
> Suddenly it is all so beautiful; the light is strange . . . Something
> about the light! He begins to cry . . .

The puppets, so delightful because they are make-believe, become metaphors for Edson's worst fears about the determinism of human life. What begins in dreamplay becomes, as it takes on a life of its own, the old nightmare of human experience, as if the toy-maker, once he has breathed life into his creation, can no more avoid witnessing its taste for wickedness than the original Toy-Maker. The dread is expressed with deadpan power in "One Morning."

One morning a man awakens to find strings coming through his
window attached to his hands and feet.

. . . I'm not a marionette, he says, his voice rising with the question, am I? Am I a marionette?

One of the strings loosens and jerks as he scratches his head.

. . . Hmmm, he says, I just wonder if I am a marionette?

And then all the strings pull and jerk and he is jumping out of bed.

Now that he's up he'll just go to the window and see who's doing
tricks with him when he's half asleep . . .

He follows the strings up into the sky with his eyes and sees a
giant hand sticking through a cloud, holding a crossbar to which the
strings are attached . . .

Hmmm, he says, that's funny, I never saw that crossbar before . . . I guess I am a marionette . . .

Dolls and puppets appear so often in Edson's poems that they seem to
have a ritual significance for him. As devices for evoking artifice and es-
tablishing parodic distance, they serve as vehicles for his dialogues with
himself through imaginative ventriloquism. He can be puppeteer or puppet
of his own words and stories. An excellent example of this is "The Little
Lady," in which a female puppet refuses to let the puppet master put his
hand under her dress. "No no, we'll have to be married first," she insists.
So he makes a puppet justice of the peace that marries them. "*Now*, and
forever, my love, she says with the puppet master making her voice with
his falsetto."

Edson has privately printed several books for his own Thing Press, but
his first widely distributed volumes were *The Very Thing That Happens*
(1964) and *What a Man Can See* (1969). It seems almost certain the latter
contains earlier work, for there is much evidence of a young poet fumbling
and then realizing where his best talent is. The earlier work resembles
campy New York writing of the fifties in the manner of Frank O'Hara,
James Schuyler, Kenneth Koch, and Barbara Guest. Only in a few of the
poems does the true originality of Edson emerge. In "The Man Rock," for
example, a "A rock awakens into a man. A man looks. A man sleeps back
into a rock as it is better for a rock in a garden than a man inside himself
trembling in red darkness." [7] Suddenly we have the mature Edson themes

7. Russell Edson, *What a Man Can See* (Penland, N.C., 1969).

in the spare style: the metamorphic drama, the combinations of absurdity and pathos, the strange humor and bitterness.

At this stage Edson called his work fables rather than prose poems. Though the label doesn't fit perfectly, it is apt. The texts are short, narrative, satiric, with overtones of allegory. For all the enjoyment of outrageousness, the morals of his best works are usually the same: that the family is an impossible community, sadistic, destructive of personal realization; that the adult world is hopelessly absurd; that nothing is what it seems, and everything capable at best of endless metamorphosis. In the face of perpetual disappointments of identity, ambition, and value, and to thwart responsibility, Edson's narrators uphold a childlike glee, a commitment to play for its own sake.

Edson's texts are compelling not so much for their morals as for the eccentric fusion of familiar and fabulous drama in concentrated wit and accurately rendered psychic warfare. Though his pathetic humor is as much akin to the backwoods comic, the tall tale, vaudeville, the shaggy dog story, and Will Rogers as it is to New York experimentalism, the economy and acid of his treatment of archetypal conflict make him an innovator. At the same time, his avant-gardist roots give him sophistication and assurance.

It is also in the early poems of *What a Man Can See* that Edson introduces his knack for making names from common nouns. Among his characters here and later are Mr. Brain, Dr. Brilliantine, Mr. and Mrs. Duck Dinner, Farmer Blink, Captain Happiness, Dr. Clutter, Clyde Bricabrac, Doctor Elephant, Dr. Funnyperson, Dr. Graciousness, and Mr. and Mrs. Blurr. These names give a comic strip immediacy and instant parodic color to his stories (Edson's father was a well-known comic strip artist), but this habit of Pop-naming characters does not always work in the poet's favor. Often the names give a glibness and thinness to the narratives, adding little after the first reading.

The families in Edson's work are not only murderous and lustful toward each other, but destructive of fantasy making. The man is enemy of the child, and the woman is enemy of both man and child. Most are horrified by their sexuality and the sexuality they see or project on the world around them. As the family represents a unit in conflict with itself, the individual is many characters, divided and confused and destructive like the family. Here anything is possible, and much of it happens.

Edson's best poems have the authority and authenticity of dreams at the playful service of a shaping faculty. Although Edson claims not to be interested in the memorability and perfection of his work, only in the act of writing it, his texts are read and rediscovered like glimpses of old dreams. The best are remembered for their precision and symmetry as well as for the story. "The Fall" is one of the plainest and shortest of the early fables in *What a Man Can See*.

There was a man who found two leaves and came indoors holding them out saying to his parents that he was a tree.

To which they said then go into the yard and do not grow in the livingroom as your roots may ruin the carpet.

He said I was fooling I am not a tree and he dropped his leaves.

But his parents said look it is fall.

Edson is best in short visits. The eccentricity and intensity of his dreaming are too much for most of us to sustain for long, and the perspective of his closet too narrow and disorienting. But in brief rounds commensurate with the curvature of his forms, he is a spellbinder and comedian beyond compare.

Fred Chappell's *Midquest*

1982

One of the rarest gifts in modern poetry is that for narrative. The legacies of imagism and modernist fragmentation seem to have stifled the special talent that can tell stories in measure. Among the poets of our time there are many with great ability for concentration of phrase and figure, for fluent improvisation with tone and allusion, and even for resonant statement. And there are many fine storytellers and novelists among us. But there is virtually no one since Frost who can do both at once. Perhaps it is the unfortunate trend toward specialization that deprives us of such versatility, or it may be the limitation of our ambitions. But part of the burden of American poetics has been the tunnel vision, not to say snow blindness, of trying to look directly upon the face of the Word and tell what it is like. In trying to be elohists of a new world, our poets have left much of the best of the imagination to the novelists.

Of course the art of prose is as difficult as any poetry, but in our culture it does not carry the same aura of ambition and expectation. Poetry is something to be worshiped from afar, not read, while it is to prose that we turn for entertainment, information, authority. We should value all the more, therefore, a writer such as Fred Chappell who can combine the two arts. He is both poet and novelist, and also a short story writer. But he is at his best in what can only be called narrative poetry. By this designation I do not mean prose broken into lines, and I will distinguish what Chappell does best by calling it a lyric narrative, implying that the local texture of the lines is as interesting and concise as lyric poetry, while the overall movement of each piece is essentially narrative. Of course there is a considerable difference between prose narrative and verse narrative. The former usually incorporates much detail and proceeds at the pace of the reader, while the latter leaves far more to implication, as in other verse, and proceeds at the slower rhythm of repeated lineation.

There is a wholeness about the work of Chappell. Everything he does seems a piece of the same cloth, whether story, poem, novel, or essay, and whatever he does fits with all the rest. It is the voice that dominates and is recognizable, no matter where you start any of his works, speaking with great richness of mind and language, deeply learned, acid at times, but always improvising, engaging whatever is at hand with all its attention, true overall to a wonderful good will and wit. Whether the subject be his parents or Linnaeus, he demonstrates the same gift for luminous phrase and detail. All his work has the tone of the gifted rememberer and tale teller delighting in his powers and flights of merrymaking memory. The voice is often self-deprecating and parodic, and the range of reference from the learned and reverent to the grotesque and mock-heroic. But there is an enormous amount of affection here for these people and their brief triumphs and losing battles with the sad facts of their lives.

Earthsleep is the last volume of a four-volume work called *Midquest,* published by Louisiana State University Press. Each volume is a separate poem, and all are spoken on the same day, May 28, 1971, the Dantean thirty-fifth birthday of the poet. Each poem, *River, Bloodfire, Wind Mountain,* and *Earthsleep,* symbolizes one of the four classical elements. The centering of these poems in all of experience, midway in a lifetime, is important in more ways than the merely chronological. While touching extremes of usage and allusion at times, the work clearly derives its élan from the middle range of experience, stressing no angle of vision over another, and rendering with utmost care and humor the lives of grandmother, parents, aging mountain Falstaffs, and storekeepers. With his fluent "prose" style Chappell has achieved a kind of middle poetry, centered in the actual, familiar as conversation, but often as wry and learnedly comic as the poetry of, say, John Crowe Ransom. He uses elaborate traditional forms for the most humble subjects, often making stil-novist terza rima a vehicle for Appalachian whoppering.

This very middleness about *Midquest* is one of its most daring features, for it enables Chappell to avoid the safe and accepted manners of so much contemporary poetry and navigate far beyond the surrealist, confessional, formalist, and agrarian limits so many contemporaries have imposed on themselves. Chappell has found a "synthetic" style that enables him to assimilate all he knows into his work. Steering a middle course, he has avoided the siren call of the safely ambiguous on the one side and the heady maelstrom of manner on the other. Starting from the harbor of a familiar port he has crossed the equator and been baptized in new tropical waters and, like the true yarn teller he is, has incorporated the new figures seamlessly into his old tales.

But having said all this I must point out that the very difference of Chappell's work puts it exactly in the tradition of American poetry. Only by turning away from the accepted poetic norms into its own eccentricities and obsessions can the American gift seem to work. It is the veering away that brings one toward the middle. Chappell follows the pattern almost exactly, turning away from the high serious and meticulously chiseled understatement of verse to an explosion of free verse, hyperbole, flamboyant experimentation with French forms, and autobiography. In the rejection of poetry for the playfulness and wrinkles of self he finds his true Poetry. In the contrasts of form and freedom, ideas and facts, sad failure and rebellious joy, we find an authentic gift.

There are formal complexities in *Midquest* that will, and should, go unnoticed until a second or third reading. The whole is interwoven and subtly counterpointed with motifs and repetitions. Characters appear and later reappear in the poems. The variety of form and tone is used as a narrative as well as a poetic pacing device. Each volume is complete in itself yet completes the whole structure, which begins with the surfacing from the unity of sleep at dawn beside Susan the wife-muse, and moves through a long day of remembering and storytelling, shaggydogging and drinksinging, and outright powerful poetry, to night and the return to unity and sleep with Susan, the earth-death muse and mother.

Part of Chappell's power is his willingness to put all of himself into this work. He gives to his poetry a great reservoir of learning, lyric hymning, science fiction and fantasy, country music ("I went walking up Chunky Gal / To watch the black bird whup the owl"). That he is willing to invest so many facets of himself is our gain, for we come to feel the wholeness of a human being. There is the recognition that this is truly a man, in the gaudy landscape of our times, yes, and seen from more angles than we normally see, and with greater focus and knowledge, but nevertheless a man in touch at times with the absurd and corny, at times with the sublime.

Midquest is about curvature and rondure, the return of that which goes out in the morning from its bed, and the turning of the earth and seasons, the sweep from the marriage of all in sleep (death) out through the almost overwhelming detail and near-chaos of experience back to the unity of love and dream. The theme is also the recurrence of everything, from the least déjà vu to the grandest rhyme of history, and the night of stars beyond human history. The central thread is perhaps the cycles of being, and each volume recapitulates the others and repeats the whole. Thus the hill in "On Stillpoint Hill at Midnight" in *River* returns near the end of *Earthsleep* in "Stillpoint Hill That Other Shore," and the Virgil Campbell of "Dead Soldiers" in the first volume returns again and again, most notably in "Firewater" of *Bloodfire* and "Three Sheets in the Wind" in *Wind Mountain* and finally in "At the Grave of Virgil Campbell" in *Earthsleep*. The curve from birth in water to the deathsleep in earth-muse is repeated in each volume as well as in the overall shape of the tetralogy. We are led through a Dante/Einstein curved and closed universe where every route and every sin and every happiness leads back to the place of beginning.

Another image that recurs is that of the Tree of Fire. The flame is, of course, man himself in the pain of his inspiration, but it reminds us of the prophet Jeremiah and his bones of fire, and of the burning bush's I AM, and at other times of the Tree of Life, and, at least once, of the burning cross of the Ku Klux Klan. The fire tree is being itself, and power, authority, wrath, suffering, and glory. It is the exhilaration and self-destruction that is being, the spirit inside the often sad and failing flesh.

Chappell is at times a mother worshiper, as in the poems to the wife-muse and earth mother and water mother, and at other times a father worshiper, as in the many fire poems and prophet hymns to power and authority. This is another instance of the middleness of the vision that enables him to incorporate so many different points of view. Blake, for example, is almost exclusively a singer of power, and Whitman, a lover of sea and earth and elusive dusks.

It is in *Bloodfire* that the central metaphor, the middle of life, becomes clear, for there we see that the thirty-fifth birthday, the being born again to the second half of one's life, means to be born to death. The implication is not that as one passes the midpoint of his life he becomes increasingly aware of approaching death; rather, it is the perception that one's life has become the process of death. Every breath is an act in the long dying back into earth. And the recognition is that life is exactly the same as death, though to be alive is the opposite of being dead.

One of the finest sections of all four volumes is "Firewood," in *Blood-fire*. It is the long-running meditation of a man splitting firewood. Here we have the best of a sure prose style with the free play and compactness of a poetic gift working together.

> Flame flame where I hit now, the cat is scared, heart
> red in the oak where sun
> climbed vein by vein to seek the cool
> wedge hard where I strike now and rose
> leaves drop off as if ruin of cloud on cloud
> fell, heart of red oak strips to sunlight,
> sunlight chopped like this to pie chunks,
> like this, solid as rock cleft rock, rock
> riven by vein and vein, ah if it were all
> so easy, to hit it & see it & feel it
> buck & come clean salmon colored,
> so clean I would eat it, this neat chop
> takes down the spine of the world . . .[1]

Parallel to the drama of the maul and wedge pours a clear stream of associations branching out in dozens of directions and then circling back to the job at hand. As Thoreau said, our firewood warms us twice. We feel the mental fever working up in the speaker as he labors. His struggle to cleave the knotty wood becomes the work of people to have their lives in spite of the recalcitrance of nature. The monologue builds up to a climax of persuasion and abuse addressed to the wood.

> . . . Matter, I'm gonna
> kick your ass all over this universe, matter has only
> to sit quiet thinking, My man, never you heard of
> passive resistance?, why that's the secret of the
> world, Mexican stand off is the closest you'll get
> to the heart's heat heart of the heart,
> why don't you try the lotus position or the string
> quartet or something equally restful, for never has

1. Fred Chappell, *Midquest* (Baton Rouge, 1981). All subsequent quotations are also from this volume.

mere fever got you anywhere or me either come
to that, we could make such beautiful silence
together if only you'd slow down & shape up & let
things as they are have their guiltless pleasures,
and man replies saying unto matter, Wassamatta
you, you talking commie now all this strike talk,
I been sentenced doncha know to create reality
by the sweat of my brow, Bible sez so, take
that you hard weird pinko freak, and with this I
bring the hammer down, and the wedge the old
hearthurter doesn't even *budge* . . .

Chappell has integrated into his epic story the details and names of
his region as no one else has. "Chunky Gal," "Greasy Creek," "Standing
Indian," do not just give a sense of local usage; they become part of the
thick texture of the style, giving at once intimacy and distance to the poetry. It is as though the speaker is of two minds at once, the mountain boy
telling of the places and people of which he is derived, and the learned and
wise poet who knows Latin, Italian, French, Neoplatonism, and quantum
mechanics. The complexity of tone is rendered most clearly in the sections
about the poet's parents, in their constant harping on the hardness of the
old days on their hardscrabble farms from the comfort of their prosperous
suburban lives. There is a parodic overtone in their monologues, a teasing,
as though the poet knows that while they do miss the sweat and poverty of
their childhoods, they are exaggerating all around. Even if they could
travel back they would not, yet probably it was not as hard as they make it
sound. This essential paradox is what Chappell communicates so affection-
ately, and it partly explains his enormous popularity in the South. No one
has rendered so accurately the sense of displacement amid so much pros-
perity, and the jealous holding on to the phrases and accents of the old as
both an amused conning of the self and an irreplaceable touchstone.

Typical of this half-serious teasing are the stories about fundamentalist
religion. The little white churches in these poems cast cold shadows over
the coves, and their preachers and doctrine are never absent long from the
mind of the speaker. Whether in the mock-heroics of the terza rima "My
Grandfather Gets Doused," or in the mock-epic alliterative line of "My

Grandfather's Church Goes Up," or in the Dantean "In Parte Ove Non E
Che Luca"—which, part translation, part original, tours hell with the
Master and finds James Dickey in the Inferno for lechery—or, finally, in
the drinking hymns of "At the Grave of Virgil Campbell," we see a mind
coming to terms with one of the terrors of its world through the jujitsu of
humor. Since the church with its work ethic and hellfire cannot be ignored, it must be defused a little with parody, while the more humble,
everyday things are treated reverently. As the mighty grandmother of
"Second Wind" says after the death of her husband:

>   . . . I heard the out-of-tune
> Piano in the parlor and knew that soon
> Aunt Tildy would crank up singing "Lo, How a Rose
> E'er Blooming."—Now I'll admit Aunt Tildy tries,
> But hadn't I been tried enough for one
> Heartbreaking day? And then the Reverend Dunn
> Would speak . . . *A Baptist preacher in my house!*
> That was the final straw. I washed my face
> And took off all my mourning clothes and dressed
> Up in my everyday's, then tiptoed past
> The parlor, sneaking like a scaredey mouse
> From my own home that seemed no more a place
> I'd ever feel at home in. I turned east
> And walked out toward the barns. I put my trust
> In common things to be more serious.

There is a spirit in this work I find remarkable, and rare in contemporary poetry. Much of what we read these days is often at best hardbitten
and stingy, sometimes downright nasty to the reader. Though Chappell is
often outrageous about himself, his family, and his neighbors, there is an
assumption of community in all his work, a sense of belonging not just to
a family and place, and to a place in terms of geography, but to the terrain
of history. It is a community in time that is implied and evoked, a world
of parents and ancestors both literal and literary, as real as the expressways
and gaudy vernacular of the present.

Interestingly enough, this sureness of who he is, in a community both
poetic and familial, gives Chappell a truer rapport with contemporary cul-

ture. His imagination lives among not only the things that were, but also the things that are. That is, to paraphrase Wallace Stevens, his gift is equal to the pressure of reality. This partly explains his popularity as a poet and as a reader of his poetry. He speaks to people as they are and as he is. The authenticity is instantly perceivable, on the page and in his voice. There is no precious regionalism here, no easy agrarian indignation, no sentimental celebrations.

Earthsleep is a self-contained unit, but comprises eleven sections. I will not try to quote extensively from it, for there are too many movements and forms to do justice to in a brief essay. But with just two or three passages I hope to show something of the range and grandness of the voice, and the personable wit. In the opening section, "Earth Emergent Drifts the Fire River," spoken to the Beatrice-wife Susan, we hear a song at daybreak as the poet and world waken from the earth of common sleep and all sharpens into articulation.

> . . . speak you,
> Tell me some elder annunciation, tell me
> History is being reborn in water, in healing water
> Rise all the cities gone down, the nations who
> Died in the fire of blood take clean new bodies,
> A silver ivy of water reclaims the broken walls,
> Unguessed Atlantises poke their streaming heads
> Out of the history books, sins of the fathers
> To lordly earth overgiven rise
> Again now transformed to the great names we feed upon,
> The fertile waters of deathsleep manure the flames.

The questioning continues for each of the four elements in a recapitulation of the structure of the book and of the previous three volumes.

But in this poem, more than in the others, May 28, 1971, is both a resurrection and a foretelling of death. The concern with mortality has been threaded into the poem in general, but here it becomes primary. Much of the book can be considered epitaphs for the poet and others, but nowhere is the subject handled with more humor and affection than in "At the Grave of Virgil Campbell." Here, in a mock-eulogy at graveside, the poet addresses his old friend in the earth.

I've been fumbling with some epitaphs
In case you want to try them on for size.
HERE LIES VIRGIL CAMPBELL—ONE MORE TIME.
How's that strike you? A little naked maybe.
Something a bit more classical perhaps?

SISTE, VIATOR.

VIRGIL CAMPBELL'S QUIET HERE.

WHO NEVER WAS BEFORE.

OR:

HERE'S THE FIRST TIME IT WAS SAID

THAT VIRGIL CAMPBELL WAS GRAVELY LAID.

OR:

EARTH, RECEIVE

YOUR PLAYFUL LOVER

TO HIS ONE SLEEP

WITH NO HANGOVER.

After a long discourse on the possibilities of the afterlife ("I *know* there's Whiskey-after-Death.") and a further recounting of Virgil's likes and weaknesses and virtues, the poem ends with a salute.

What's this, it's not a hymn it's a drinking song,
Well, sometimes who can tell the difference?

To hell with the ragshank preachers
    Who made it out sinful to think,
And down with the dustdyed teachers
    Whose veins run Bible-black ink,
And Damn every one of those creatures
    Who told us we oughtn't to drink!
If ever they'd taken a sip
    (From me and Chris Sly
    Here's mud in their eye!)
They'd had more brains and less lip.

But here's to the happy old souls
    Who trip about clinking their chains
In time to the music that rolls

From the locker of Davy Jones,
And here's to the Hand that controls
  Raw-Head-&-Bloody-Bones!
Let's have us a neat little nip
  (For we and the Host
  Forever cry, "Prosit!")
Before we take our last sleep.

Let's put on our nightcaps of moonshine
  And kneel and mumble our prayers,
In Glory we drunkards will soon shine
  Singing our spiritous airs.
And, tipsy as possums by noontime,
  We'll roll down Pisgah like bears!
So pour us a tight little drop
  (And here's to the Splendor
  Of the Holy Bartender!)
And we're ready at last for our nap.

"The Peaceable Kingdom of Emerald Windows" is almost an edenic
roll call of the lovers and progeny of the earth, so colorful and rich in
allusion it turns out to be heaven, or at least an earthly paradise, that is
described. The word that comes to my mind most often as I read here is
Celtic, because of the intensity and animism of the image swirl.

Chortlings of the green uproar of Earth,
Tree-dream, weed-dream, the man within the tree,
Woman within the weed, babies inhabit
Tea roses, at the bottom of the trumpet
of day lily lies the yellow tabby cat,
Blackberry vine a whirlpool of green blaze,
And kudzu the Great Wall of China, oppossum
Of apple, plum tree is a sea urchin here
By the bridge of hills, crown of whitethorn bleeds
The broken sigh of hills, the hills launch here
Windows windows, summer dream is a freshet
Of windows, raindrop how much window, raindrop
An eye of glass, it is a window of

> Deep sadness, it is the lover's tear of goodbye,
> Goodbye I perceive to be a human creature.

Matching the wonder of landscape, beast, and flower in "The Peaceable Kingdom of Emerald Windows" is the weird threat of "My Grandmother's Dream of Plowing," in which the beloved grandmother of the earlier poems recounts a nightmare. From a new-plowed furrow she picks up a great lump of gold that turns into a goblin child "With an evil smile." She first holds it to her breast and then, frightened of the thing, wishes it would die. And no sooner does she wish than it does die, and she is left with the guilt of the murderous wish. The narrator intrudes at the end:

> "And then you woke," I said, "to the world you love."
> "And now I know," she said, "I never woke."

Near the end the book rounds back toward the sleep of earth. In the short-line free verse song called "Stillpoint Hill That Other Shore," which moves in and out of elegiac dactyls and is addressed again to Susan, the poet hymns the kinship and union of all in earth and on earth. It is a kind of marriage song, of all with the planet, and all with all.

> This hill above our house,
> stillpoint before
> the turning begins again,
> earth solid to the hand,
> earth moveless in time,
> comprised
> of the husk and marrow of
> our dead forefathers.
> Unmoving in time,
> only the dead are incorrupt.
> *Time I shall not serve thee.*
> *You earth I have loved most blest.*
>
> . . . .
>
> The peace that shall seize us
> in sleepgrip,
> that peace shall I tell you

be all the black frenzies of our flesh
in one green cuddle,
let us descend to our house
our bed
and invite the mornings,
the infinite anniversary mornings,
which reach out to touch us
with the hands of one another.

The long poem and journey through all the elements, through dreams and waking memory, through comic chorus and mock sermon, end in the conjugal sleep of all earth, in lovesleep. All sink (rise) into that paradise, beyond the gaudy and hypocritical, beyond the postures and the purgatories of wakeful work and guilty dread. The very last section is the song from earth itself, among the planets and starry coordinates fading at dawn.

Let it then be flesh that we take on
That I may see you
Cool in time and blonde as this fresh daybreak.

No one no one sleeps apart
Or rises separate
In the burning river of this morning
That earth and wind overtake.

The way the light rubs upon this planet
So do I press to you,

Susan   Susan

The love that moves the sun and other stars
The love that moves itself in light to loving
Flames up like dew

Here in the earliest morning of the world.

III

mystery and memory ─────────────────────────

The Transfigured Body:
Notes from a Journal

1970–1975

It has often been said that the southern mountains contain history in the present, are inhabited by our living ancestors. Though I grew up there I had no inkling of this until I went away to college. My area didn't quite enter the twentieth century until about 1945. I discovered an immediate rapport with the generation of Dreiser, Anderson, and Faulkner, much more than with my friends from the suburbs. What I knew was the yearning to break from the farm and small town, from the fundamentalist faith, into secular self-knowledge and expression. But at the same time I was equally drawn back to that ground along the withers of the Blue Ridge, to Old Man Early singing hymns under the oak while we worked in the fields, to the family closeness around the kerosene lamps, to the promise of signs and wonders and the land my people had cleared. The result is that I've never been much at home either with the present or with the elders. Forced to leap from the nineteenth century to now in about a decade and a half I have no lasting urge to settle in the present. This lack of affinity with fashions and generational trends may be a source of my obsession with finding absolute structures in language that mirror the everlastingness of natural process. Destruction releases us to overtake and surpass, reconstruct and revolutionize.

I have nothing more to lose. The present is soon the flapper tattooed on the old sailor's arm. I don't feel married to her.

The southern Blue Ridge has a physiognomy unlike any other mountains I have seen. Instead of long running ridges and folds, as in the Alleghenies and Poconos, there is a churned-up look, like turbulence frozen into rock and soil. They've been worn down some of course, but the beaten, tortured look is still there under the haze and lavender forests. This difference in features occurred to me years before I read that the Blue Ridge is not part of the original plate of the American continent, but was squeezed up from deep in the mantle and then pinched off by the Atlantic crust, so it's really a kind of island of foreign soil floating on the continent, still manifesting its messy origins. There is a rightness in that terrain I've always meant to explore, but so far it has eluded me just at the point of definition. I think it has something to do with the chaos out of which ideas and images arise, an unsettled and unsettling region where the poet has to live. But there's something even more personal and specific than that. In those random hog-backs and hollows there is a bodying of the mountaineer's insularity and confusion I want to both lose and discover. There is something so primitive about the southern mountains, previous to language, a shy madness, and distrust of the workable.

But in that erosioned sprawl is something the rest of America lost after the Civil War. In the backwardness and isolation a piece of the American in-nocence was kept alive. Which brings me to the kind of paradox I keep finding in poetry and ideas and nature. The marginal and chaotic have promoted more permanence than the institutions of the majority. Perhaps in inarticulateness there is hope for language and poetry, because it is more accurate to experience, and closer to possibility. Out of desperation comes the recklessness to get near enough to chaos for some fire, and out of alienation the patience to husband and direct it for the community.

All creation is evolution. Nothing comes from nothing. The great leaps are chance, mutation. We learn by watching others to be ourselves. Poems grow out of the infinite chain of poems by way of spontaneous accident, just as any image of nature is one in a catenation of images. So we have at once change and repetition, the rhyming of things, refrains, litany, all pri-meval as turbulence perhaps: day and night, the copulative return of orbits, heartbeat, the more subtle periods of comets, sunspots every eleven years, ice ages, shifting poles. We are frightened and thrilled by wrenching the habits we live by.

Any self-conscious return to Culture is deadening, and any attempt at classical orthodoxy is a deadend. Our few great poets have plowed ahead into the wilderness of their potential much as our ancestors took the continent, clearing and farming, then abandoning. Modernism and avant-gardism were homages to art itself, and proved empty. Our poetics are rooted in the Reformation, in the failure into knowledge through individual experience. Our ancestors came here originally to be alone and pray. For them each family was a separate monarchy, each man his own king and pope. This places terrific responsibility on the integrity of the solitary man.

The genius of Whitman was to make his body significant. That may be the single great leap of modern poetry. He discovered his own body as the signature of the nation, race, even soul. He would have us see his own flesh as the image of democracy. But what is the second important image of Whitman, the poet of the mass? It is the hermit thrush, the solitary singer. That is because the bedrock, the skeleton underneath that Adamic flesh, was an agonizing puritan guilt that actually surfaces in "As I Ebb'd. . . ." First and last he thought of himself as speaking in isolation. There he is also the great poet of America, languaging not only the solitude of cedar swamps and Long Island beaches, but the traplines and soddies of the West, and even the terrible privacy of New England bedrooms. For our democratic ideals and individualism we have paid from the beginning in the currency of separateness and silence. And those in the southern highlands, perhaps more than any, retreated to their isolated coves and stayed there, daring the world to invade.

Science is our new language for talking about experience. The scope of its challenge to a poet could be frightening, except that science is just vocabulary. It is our job to discover its human grammar, just as Homer must have used the Greek myths and Dante dramatized Aquinas. But when talking about science it is good to remember that the humble and ordinary are the most eligible to be exalted through language.

I would like to bring back the lyric with its directness and simplicity from its abduction by folk musicians, but at the same time I am also interested in something else, something riding on vernacular forms, texts, transcriptions, only a distant cousin to the dance of the lyric. Where the dance is more in the meaning than in the meter. Poetry has served for me as a kind of anamnesis, a recalling of something past that serves as communion between me and others. Every writing is an act of faith in the past, and in others. A poem is as close to a perpetual motion machine as we have gotten. Once completed it seems to rebuild and refuel itself in other times and places, to acquire lives of its own from readers and evolve through the changes in ways the author never imagined. In this way I think of a poem not as the word made flesh but as the flesh transfigured. Because though we don't understand poetry's origins, we know that it comes from inside us as a sensual body of language that lifts, as in a state of desire, into something else than just body, or words. Who would say that he is incarnating some myth, dogma, ghost, or law? That is not the work given us at this time. It is for us to spiritualize the body and nature since those are precisely what we have. We must translate science by recreating the integrity of things, as celebration and praise. Our gift is audience, voyance. Even a death chant is celebration, for especially when faced with absolute nothingness there is only a turn to praise to give meaning.

Since most poets have a tendency to turn their strengths into weaknesses by imitating themselves, by parodying themselves, by running into the ground whatever gifts they discover, I want to make of my weaknesses something strong. My shakiest faculty is talk, and I will start there and see where it takes me. I think my reticence evolved because my people in the old days were Pentecostal Holiness, not orthodox Baptists. They spoke in tongues and shouted at revival meetings. They were disliked by and disliked the dryhides. An aunt danced a holy dance at my grandmother's funeral. This strain is to me shameful, celebrative, a little mad, a not quite respectable reaching for something beyond. I know now that I will always be a little embarrassed by that aspect of poetry, will always keep one hand in the quiet banter of the country store and one in the fierce aspiration of the brush arbor.

But poetry is in another place. It is the serene white pines after the discomforts of church and society. It is to a great extent to my mother that I owe a delight in the commonplace and nondramatic, a calm and lucid feeling for things in their fullness that I found in my own writing. I remember following her as a very young child looking for bird nests in the grass along the field and gathering mustard greens in March. And I remember her mother also, who kept me until I was three, and can still see the tines of frost on the grass where she milked in the early morning after my mother had gone to the cotton mill.

The energy of poetry, contrary to popular myth, is a great deal more erotic and apollonian than bacchic, not intoxicated and weakened. For the Greeks, Apollo was the god of poetry, not Bacchus. It is as if we are persuaded that the great religious madmen like Blake and Smart were writing out of drunkenness instead of their craving for clarity and eternal truth. But there is a drunkenness far less benign than alcohol. Poets tend to become intoxicated with the sound of their own voices. They talk on and on believing that anything they say is valuable because they have talent. This is a part of the general tendency toward narcissism in our time. I don't think any of us quite understand it.

We suffer from a rampant inflation, in language as well as economy. Words are cheap, and ideas, and tropes. The poetry is lost in a polysyllabic mist of parody and easy wit. And we would avoid the cure of depression if possible. I think it was Alistair Cooke who said he saw much enthusiasm in America but little creativity. Why must our time dictate mediocrity? Is it the welfare state of mind, generated by government grants, writing programs, reading circuits, the bureaucracy of art? Surely it is not that simple. But we have not made the artificial insemination of poetry really work. I understand that we must gather wherever we can to have community, that writing programs are here to counter the loneliness and space of America, that we feel there is no other place to go in these inflationary times. But the professionalism has proven self-defeating. Our institutions work like centrifuges flinging the heaviest material into the hinterlands, and keeping the lightest and most insubstantial near the centers, close to the whirling vacuums.

Though the poet cannot be innocent, but authentically fallen from his first ideals, he will be nothing without innocence. He must be able to discover, even as he forgets, that the body is spirit, the phenomenon the noumenon. The thrust of poetry is beatific, affirmative. Even from ashes we make mortar. The imagination is amphibious, able to live in two different states at once, innocence and knowledge, the sublime and the carrious.

Be the poet of informed humility, the elohist of topsoil. Maybe it's time to say to hell with literature, and start over again with whatever obsesses you. Just by speaking I am scion to the whole trunk and root system of language and history. Don't forget the poem's carnality. I want to dramatize nature, the vegetal, the unsayable.

It is objectivity and precision that can be translated and that translates, the love of humble detail, a sensitivity to the eros in all things, focused recognition.

The timing of a poem is terribly important. It is the *coming together* (sexual) of diverse and opposing bits of information, insight. Every good writer knows the importance of chance, and that genius is the ability to seize inherent possibilities in anything at all as they hint to you. Cleverness in itself can be valuable to a poet but is not necessary. The quickness of poetry is not the same as quickness of wit. The poet is one of the few people of our time who have the patience *to get it right*. In an age that must be dominated by mass production and expediency just to feed the populations of the world and provide the comforts they demand and will demand, only someone not supplying consumers has the chance to see through to completion. The poet's advantage is that he is an amateur in a world of professionals. His product is not necessary. Nothing depends on his finishing a poem this afternoon or twenty years from now. He has the ultimate opportunity for saying what he means, and finding just what it is he has to say. Too-active pursuit of a career can forfeit a great part of this freedom and privilege. I cannot say strongly enough, in the face of present trends, that the poet is not just a technician, a card-carrying journeyman who solves practical problems in communication, who reaches a competency and is certified.

What we keep looking for is a poetic space to discover and explore. This extension and deepening of actual space is a primary function of language. At the most immediate level it could be called escapism, but more accurately it is a focusing of all the faculties and energies at once to punch out an opening in the wall of habit. Perhaps I should say both new space and new time since poetry provides a leap out of the self-conscious continuum into measure, and beyond that into something even nearer to absolute than music. All the best construction is reconstruction, revisioning. There is no Edenic space, only the attentive re-creation of leftovers, fragments, a resurrecting into potent form.

I once wrote a passage in a longer poem in which I compared cultural institutions such as universities to fish ladders around big obstructions, where in just a few hundred yards the salmon mount higher than in a hundred miles of stream. And suddenly in that great body of accumulation, the repository of knowledge and know-how, it is difficult to find the feeder streams whose mouths are buried in the rich bottom mud. There is no way to begin working toward the headwaters and personal accomplishment, realization. The reservoir is perfect for smaller lake fish that don't migrate from deep in the ocean to just under the mountaintops.

To be an agrarian implies a belief in the permanence of past institutions. I believe in the anarchic and creative soil, and stick to the fringes of society, out where it comes into collision with nature, in the chaotic backwashes and countereddies.

Our best talent has been a healthy irreverence for art and a reverence for energy in instance. But why limit ourselves to mere textures and vague associations? It takes courage to be clear about what you're doing. There is the risk. Like the original creator the poet makes for his own glory, and he hates to stake his potential on anything particular, though only the specific can generate the aura when he's no longer around.

A democracy of intellect, yes. But what is a democracy of poetry? Is it the right to fail? Has there ever been anything else? Certainly we need to get beyond ego poetry, and recent scholastic poetry. A learned prosiness has always been deathly for the imagination trying to rise above the level of exercises or cut beneath, and tends more toward duncing than dancing. Since the American poems have been powered by our sense of pioneering verbal and ideal territories we have no gnostic tradition, except maybe Poe, and a fine thread running through the work of Emily Dickinson. Our strength of straightforwardness, rising out of the Reformation, may also be a weakness. Even Whitman warned that the poet comes upon his best by indirection.

It is our delight to animate and spiritualize even as nature has animated the elements and made them cognitive. Years ago I wrote in a note that poetry always points in the direction of the ultimate metaphor, suggesting that in some fantastic way everything is the same thing. This recognition of kinship is maybe the central thrust of poetry, the basis of celebration, but like all main currents in the psyche it should be antagonized, resisted until it overwhelms. For the poet must be in the crow's nest and boiler room at once, and not only at the helm, which implies a cybernetic function shouting down the imagination. Once driving through the piedmont countryside in a drowsy mood I realized what the key to my writing was to be. I saw that if I followed a certain principle I couldn't fail. It was incredibly simple. But by the time we had stopped for ice cream at a country store and driven home, I had forgotten, as I sat down to write, just what the realization had been. And I haven't been able to recall it since, luckily.

The failure of any one poet may benefit poetry as much as any success. One's running on a dead end may strengthen the main stem as pruning certain branches confirms and extends the growth of a fruit tree. Poetry like everything else is a tincture, a resolving. Language can avatar experience. That interests me. I want a periscopic reach, to stay on the ground yet see from above. Or snorkel a breath from the upper air from my quotidian mud.

I write to establish the reality of things. It's as if I'm afraid they aren't there unless substantiated by language, and consubstantiated. I need the confidence of a street preacher who can go on shouting to oblivious traffic. American poets have written both the country and the city, but no one seems to know what to do with the suburbs and bedroom towns. There must be something so unreal about spending huge chunks of our days commuting in a kind of limbo that we are inarticulate. Perhaps the true location of the suburbs is television, not any terrain.

It is ironic that the poetics of common speech and ordinariness have alienated the wide audience of poetry even further. The popular ideal of poetry remains roughly neoclassical, stilted, artificial. Check any poetry corner of a small town newspaper. Plain speech sounds like poetry only to the poets.

We must not lose the ability to distinguish between the interestingly written text and the stroke of lightning. It's true that in poetry as in angling "the big ones almost always get away." And we keep stocking the depleted streams of fashion with millions of fry hoping everyone will take home a token catch.

The poet like Antaeus gets strength from touching the ground. His danger is not flying, but living too much in houses and offices. In the confusions and disorientations, the backtrackings and veerings of consciousness, we should be at once ascetics and sensualists, at once terrified and confident enough on the psychic rollercoaster to keep our eyes open. I feel most active when asleep. A poem is structured freedom, appetitive.

Usually it's when I've given up on writing altogether, forgotten it, that a good poem comes along. Attention is often renewed by what we despise and reject. The poem comes from somewhere else, and from where we have been looking all along without seeing it. Writing with just the senses is miserly accumulation, the poem as piggy bank.

Poetry arises from the aspiration toward ideal forms. Open, innovative forms are impossible without commensurate ideals, would be empty shells, mere textures and surfaces. Short of that level of inspiration poems gain authority only by tapping the strength of traditional forms.

Crops are grown, not in the marketplace or fortress, but in the outlying country, in open fields.

Mica: Reflective Bits from Notebooks

1970

Language must lead beyond language.

Good poetry in our time is almost invisible. It exists all around but is virtually unseen, hidden by the noise of modern life, and the media. Poetry has always had to exist at the fringe of American culture. Poets have no role in the mind of the public, as they seem to have in France and Russia, for example.

Poetry exists in the speech of the nonindustrialized people around us, and to a smaller degree in all speech. But you must know what to listen for to find it.

Poetry is here (unseen by most) and always will be because it is a process, not just some words on a page. As long as people speak they will need the energy of poetry to distill and heighten speech, to delight and move them.

Most ideas, feelings, in fact, civilization, are carried in words, in language, and we cannot afford to let it erode.

1971

Failure makes you aware of the death growing in your flesh. But at the very instant of pain we see everything clearly, as in the illumination of lightning's brief maps. Yet, whatever the failure, at some point you find you can go on; things open up again, the oxygen is still there.

1976

Why all this strain of death in our American vision? Is it akin to the awful loneliness of the Puritan conscience, the full weight of godliness, the self-reliance of faith demanding that each assume the mantle of divinity and suffering, the burden of first sin? Did the very closeness of the soil generate the fixation? The quaking bogs all covered with moss and lichens, rotten logs like coffins in the balsam woods, the swamps and remote tarns? Even Poe fits that paradigm, but in his own self-carved interior of gothic splendor. Williams was right about his authenticity.

We are a continent discovered by going west to reach the sacred, legendary East, suggesting perhaps that our best motions are backwards, counter-motions, the tacking done by reverse English, so to speak. Every good poem is a kind of declaration of independence, a fusing of ideal and literal. Our reaction to old England forks with the gothic inwardness of Poe and the expansive idealism of Emerson.

Again, we back into our originality, warping upstream to the wide interior, to the rhetoric of the New Testament, especially Revelation. Mention the Pilgrim longing for a plain life of spiritual richness, say something about the great wilderness as fact, the distance as symbol of the separation of individual from individual. Talk of facts as messages from the soul. Talk about privacy and solitude, the trapper's hut, the shaggy tracts of claimed land. Talk about land-hunger, starvation for space of the European poor, the cult of the primitive, the real love/hate for the Indian.

In our country we have often hoped for the primitive and mythic, only to reveal our decadence. What spiritual carnality we aspire to, only to find carnality. Through our vernacularity we hope to discuss the subtle and elevated, make unity of the clutter, raise the jargon of science to a sacred language, and end too often with abstraction, flatness.

Our most common modern form is autobiography, confession, self-analysis, allied to the peculiar narcissism of so much contemporary art. The danger is that with no audience, and no hope of an audience, poets will write only to themselves. My horror is of much action and little originality. Better creative indolence.

Language is by its very nature affirmative, because the act of articulating, even anger, violent emotion, is controlled response. Suicide-prevention agencies know that talk is the first step toward will and work. The elemental sentence is the forwarding of energy from one point of being to another. Language is in a literal sense constructive, requires an act of making. It is at once constructive and destructive, as is perception itself. Language is the shaping of breath, implying deeper syntax beyond speech. Language is the understructure of the collective imagination.

Poetry moves both in and out of time as it occupies space and rears back toward original form. The two motions are functions of each other, and the distance between them is the thickness and depth of the poem. The music of poetry derives more from economy, quickness, accuracy, than from meter or even the natural rhythm of the sentences. The mere music of language is rather dull. But the spare sentence muscled with substance resounds, and cools gravity.

Nothing works in poetry better than narrative, or at least the hint of narrative. It lights up even ordinary images and phrasing. Get the tension by story, get the attention by tension. Something must be happening in poetry as in fiction. The very nature of language is narrative, the relation of something going on, subject, verb, object.

But poetry moves and delights us in short passages, almost never in whole poems, at least almost never in poems of any length. It is those sparks of detail and music that we remember and return to. And the sense of wholeness and authority implied by the fragments.

Poetry is elision, a leaving out. I don't want to be a sharecropper with the harvest I take from the soil. I would rather give all away. I want word-telescopes, not hairshirts of wisdom. I go for mythic realism, real icons. A poem must witness the collision of two or more ideas to generate energy. The shape of the conflict can be formal (fencing) or freestyle (wrestling).

I do not believe in deifying the imagination. Such stress on process seems technical and limited. I like askewness as much as symmetry, and don't want to starve the vulgar life-giving faculties by worshiping imagination. Poetry seems to be written best on the brink of chaos, where it draws from turbulence but is free enough to cool into form.

1978

Poetry is always a turning, and a turning back. Trope, figure. Never a proceeding in the logical and programmatic, never an agenda. Poetry is the verso, the reverse side of any image, the surprise reversal. Poetry does not argue, it discovers and affirms. It begins with the fact and names the unnamable. Look to the least poetic subject for paydirt, and to the least poetic language.

Mind generates language to prove it will never die.

An image is a language tensor, the compact union of two separate systems of reference. The pharaoh's dream of riding in a crystal.

I would take the filth and stinky cans and sawdust bags, soot and broken bulbs, and crush the mess into a compact ingot, into a fleshy diamond.

One acre will eat a family.

The fictional integrity of a poem should not be violated by mouthing about its composition. If we are reading a text we know it is text, not actual experience.

It's the gap in the circuit that makes the welding fire, that cuts the hardest steel, and joins seamlessly.

It is the time just before discovery that we look back on with such feeling, such nostalgia, creating now the missed expectancy. The present grows on the rubbish and unfinished business of the past. Decadence makes the richest soil. Our times are well manured.

Poetry awakens what is most other and yet most ourselves.

1991

I wonder about the influence of TV commercials on poetics. Nothing in our culture is so finely honed, so elegantly compressed. Children go around quoting commercials the way children of former times chanted nursery rhymes. At a cost of many thousands of dollars per second commercials have to do their work quickly, through the surprising image, the implicit narrative of romance, aspiration. And they must stick in the memory. They suggest the vivid fragment that is the model of so much contemporary poetry. And yet the commercial is completely without depth, without the reach of poetry.

It is not the "chaos" of contemporary life that is so notable, but rather the predictability, the routines. Our lives are organized down to the second, our days and weeks and years planned to the hour. In spite of all the talk of uncertainty and loss of belief, people are perhaps surer of who they are and where they fit in creation than ever before, thanks to science and psychoanalysis. It may indeed be the mystery of existence they miss most, a world haunted by forces beyond their understanding.

Could the randomness, the rubato, the very freedom of free verse, be a rebellion against the tidiness of so much contemporary life? In truly chaotic times, in a world of threat and catastrophic change, the predictability of regular versification would be welcomed, as a way of containing, and seeming to control, the welter of experience, the colliding systems of understanding.

In any case, it is no excuse for poetry that it merely mirrors the confusion of its times. A landfill would serve as well. As it is no excuse for obscure poetry that it can be explained. One danger of the academic environment has always been that it values the gloss over the poem. The primary business of poetry is delight, complex delight and praise, whether hex or haecceity.

The ruled space of a great poem is a kind of periodic chart, implying in compact symbols a whole universe, animated, elusive, changing, even while arranged in lattices permanent as crystal. As all history is implicit in language, so all matter is implicit in each element, and all voices in each vowel. Each branch speaks a dialect of water, but evokes the ocean.

Look at a poem written a decade ago, the page yellowed and covered with dust. Does a line shine through, a single word? Does a thought there live beyond the writer's enthusiasm in the act of making? Is there exhilaration of the intersection of time and eternity? When the dust is brushed away, what breathes, what demands to be spoken again?

IV

the wisdom of work ————————————————

Interview by Jeff Daniel Marion

JDM: Are there specific individuals who have been important guides for you in your writing? Individuals who've opened you to possibilities?

RM: I suppose the most honest answer would be to start off and say yes, many teachers and friends have of course had a great influence on me and my writing, but that more than any literary work or personality the force and presence of my parents in the beginning have shaped the kind of poetry I write and would like to write.

In many ways their influence was always contradictory and for that reason invigorating. (I have discovered since I left home that mountain families are much closer than the average American family. I had no way or need to know that when I was growing up, but it's true. The family is really the only social organization in the mountains, and all relationships almost are family relationships.) But there were such differences within the family. For instance there was and is the presence of my father, a well-read man with little formal education, a brilliant talker, who I'm sure turned me toward an early love of language. He always dominated conversations, in the field, at prayer meetings, around the fireplace. I've seen him stand by the road and talk to a friend stopped in his car for hours. I would have to go beg him to come so we could eat. He and his family leaned away from the Southern Baptists toward the Pentecostal Holiness church, and he often took part in the services of various splinter groups in private homes, shouting and speaking in tongues. I was both terrified and fascinated by all this, and out of it I think I acquired a resistance to the orthodox and established, a distrust of formality, a taste for the rebellious and New Testament ecstatic. My father is a huge man, ill at ease in polite society, preferring to be off with a friend or two working and talking.

Contrastingly my mother, though not really a quiet person, taught me a sense of delight in the small and ordinary. It is that I have developed most in my poems, what I have often referred to as the "Chinese mountaineer" sensibility, a calm and lucid feeling for things in their objective fullness. . . . My mother, who has had a very hard life, much death and long sickness in her family, and who always worked to help support us, has a tremendous strength and reserve and even tranquility that I find awesome.

Beyond the early relationships I find the strictly literary influences seem relatively small. But I would like to add that the poetry and fiction of Fred Chappell, and his encouragement, have had a great impact on later years. His novel *The Inkling* is a minor classic, well known in France and England, though not as much in America. He is a great teacher, with something of the same genius Pound had for spotting talent and drawing it out. When I went off to college I remember feeling pretty much lost among the upper middle class types I met there. But Fred was from my part of the state, and talked the way I did. More than anyone he taught me the craft of words. I have several letters that he wrote from Florence in 1968 about poems I was sending to him, which I treasure.

JDM: How would you define your sense of place?

RM: I spent the first sixteen years of my life on our farm near Zirconia. There's about a square mile of land there I know every foot of. It was bought by my great-great-grandfather back in 1840 and though now divided into remnants among the descendants (some of it has been sold out of the family), I was privileged to tramp and play on all of it. I think my sense of place is very local indeed, not a culture, not a region, just one community. Since moving away I have found myself comparing everything I've seen to that archetypal acreage, soil, plants, climate, stream beds, as well as people. This strong attachment to one particular piece of ground is both an advantage and a liability in our times. There is that solidity there, a home, a place to go back to no matter what happens. But that very tie can make you uneasy and a little alien in the other places you're bound to move to in our nomadic times. It took years for me to learn to write about other places and people. I'm still working on it. In America today there's a great fluidity and uncertainty that I find creative. I feel part of that too, and sometimes think I can see it more clearly than my friends who grew up in the suburbs.

One feature I keep returning to about the area around Zirconia is the mining. All over our property there are pits and depressions where my ancestors dug for zircons or explored for lead, or mica, or gold. The tiny stream below our barn called Kimble Branch yields a trace of gold, and during the Civil War it was panned repeatedly. In the 1890s Edison and a mineralogist named Hidden opened a large zircon mine two miles east of our place and hired locals to work it. They hauled away tons of low-grade gems to make zirconium for their filaments. (I had relatives named Edison Staton and Hidden Freeman.) The image of a filament has always fascinated me, slender structures that through resistance to the current candesce and illuminate. Of course it takes just the right amount of resistance to the flow of things, in poems and in life; too much and the whole system burns out, too little and there's no heat generated. That and dams, which also obstruct the natural flow and transform it into power, channeling trillions of raindrops say, harvesting both sun and gravity.

It might be interesting to mention that electricity was just coming to our valley when I was a child. I remember well the old kerosene lamps that are now back in fashion. The hintervalleys of our creek were not lighted until about the time I left for college. My friends around Cornell often tease me that I'm really eighty years old, instead of thirty, having lived through technological development that in the rest of the country stretches roughly over the period since World War I. Before I was eight my father had neither car nor pickup and we hauled corn out of the field with the horse and wagon, and used them to gather creek rock for our new house.

One of the less pleasant legacies of the Blue Ridge is the painful sense of insularity and alienation the mountain people feel, or did then, even a sense of inferiority to the rest of the country. In my county this was heightened by the presence of many wealthy lowlanders in the nearby Flat Rock area, going back to the 1820s, who summered in the mountains and sometimes hired my relatives for menial jobs. And in my time by the thousands of tourists that drove in from Florida and the rest of the Deep South. Nothing can make you feel more backward than hundreds of Miami Cadillacs among the pickups of your hometown, and the smart-talking harangue of the slickers trying to get your produce cheap.

I understand one of the great problems of such cities as Cincinnati and Chicago now is the influx of people from Appalachia. It is a national tragedy that these people have been economically forced off their land into the urban hell. No good will ever come of their exile in the ghettos.

JDM: Do you feel you are a voice for a particular place?

RM: It would be pretentious of me to say that I feel I am the voice of any area or people. On the other hand if I'm any good as a writer it will be because I speak what others know and feel but don't say. A poet if he's really great becomes the spokesman for his whole race or nation. What I worry about is saying it my way; if that's done well enough it aligns with what others see and would say too. I have tried to create verbal spaces in which other *things* and animals, not just people, can be heard. Maybe what I've tried to voice most is how natural things and manmade things decay and endure: institutions, artifacts, the dirt. For a long while I've been working at a little poem called "Tear Bottle," where I compare my writing to a nutshell of brine, "Wept by the saints of my childhood for law / and changes."

JDM: What sort of obligations or commitments does this sense of place bring?

RM: I think a certain loyalty to the mud and trash around us can help the poet deal with the narcissism and prosiness rampant in so much verse we see these days.

There is something releasing about moving through language outside yourself into unlikely places and vantages. Dealing directly with the briar patch and gullies of waste can divert the ego, triggering, at least for me, a rush of imagination. My prime obligation or commitment is to communicate that surge of feeling that comes when the ordinary stuff around us is seen anew.

Interview by Suzanne Booker

1984

SB: Since this issue is devoted to North Carolina writers, and since your southern Appalachian heritage contributes so forcefully to your themes and subjects, would you tell me more about growing up in Zirconia?

RM: I'm not sure how important the place where one grows up is to poetry, except as setting, background. It's after all the quality of the writing, the art and the vision, that make poetry interesting, not the scenery and locale, not even the subject matter. But one of the particular things about growing up when I did in Henderson County, North Carolina, was that I was able to see a community change rapidly and forever. I was raised on a farm that had been in the family since 1840, and very few of my cousins and uncles had ever left the valley, except to work temporarily on construction jobs, or to go into the army. It was a life that revolved around farming and family and church. You were related by blood to almost everyone you knew.

But at the same time you were aware of the isolation, partly because so many tourists were coming to western North Carolina even then. The wealthy of Charleston and Atlanta had used Henderson County as a summer resort since the 1820s, and there was that strange juxtaposition of the local people with the low country rich.

So there was a great contrast, of sophistication and poverty side by side. Paradox and change are always enriching to the imagination. Perhaps I was lucky in that way. But I never felt quite at home in Zirconia, even as a child. Industry was moving in from the North, and new families were buying land and sending their children to the schools. It was scary and exciting. . . .

What is impossible to communicate to my contemporaries in the worlds of universities and poetry is the awful sense of remoteness and difference you have growing up in a little cove of the Blue Ridge Mountains. When I've tried to write about that sense of *outsideness* I've been accused of exaggerating, of bragging. What is most literal and accurate in my writing has often been taken to be fantastic. I have a friend who's the heir to a considerable corporate fortune, who has often said to me, "Of course you're from the middle class just like the rest of us." And I always smile and nod. It astonishes me when reviewers question, not my art, but my veracity. It's as though they're upholding the very difference I was trying to communicate.

SB: Why are there so many good poets in North Carolina?

RM: It's a fairly recent thing: the North Carolina writers we have early in the century, Thomas Wolfe and Paul Green, had a fabulous reputation. I was astonished the other day to think about Paul Green and just how famous he was. He's pretty much forgotten now, but he won a Pulitzer Prize in 1927 when he was in his early thirties. Thomas Wolfe was the most famous writer in America about 1930, and the Playmakers had presented all his first plays in Chapel Hill. Then for a long time you don't have much happening in North Carolina, until the sixties when people like Reynolds Price and Doris Betts, John Ehle and Fred Chappell, came along. It was just in the last decade and a half that there were many poets from North Carolina; it's astonishing and thrilling. I certainly don't know the explanation for it. Yet what impresses me is the variety: everybody from Jonathan Williams, representing a very individual sort of Black Mountain style of poetry, to Ammons, another highly individual style. Fred Chappell, Bill Harmon (he's certainly his own kind of poet), me, James Applewhite, Michael McFee, Betty Adcock, and I've left out a half a dozen people publishing nationally. It must have something to do with the way North Carolina has been a collision place for cultures; it's South, but it's upper middle South. In the sixties when I was in college it was a place changing so rapidly, and I think that is always good for poetry.

SB: You've cited your parents as also important in shaping the kind of poetry you write.

RM: Of course it goes without saying, in these post-Freudian times, that everyone is deeply influenced by his parents. We're just what our mothers made us, one of my colleagues keeps saying. But as I get older I realize more and more what strong personalities my parents were and are. Though without benefit of formal education they are both readers, my mother of fiction and my father of history and the *National Geographic Magazine*. Both have always read constantly in the Bible, and they read to my sister and me every night when we were little. I used to listen to Evangeline's lesson—she was three years older than me—and by the time I was six I could read all her books. Because I was born in October I couldn't attend school until almost seven, but my mother taught me at home and I knew arithmetic and reading well before the first grade.

My mother was always interested in natural things, in looking for herbs and flowers, in the names of medicinal roots and barks, and she often pointed out hummingbirds and nests, tiny things. I think I share that love of the minuscule, the intricate and intimate. Her mother, whom I remember a little, had known the names of all wild things and passed much of her memory on to her. My mother worked in cotton mills, beauty shops in town, and in an electrical plant, but she never lost her delight, even passion, for gardening. When young she had memorized poems from textbooks and magazines and she used to recite them.

My father is the talker in the family. Where I'm the introvert, he's the extrovert. His mother and grandfather had belonged to the Pentecostal Holiness movement in the 1890s, and he himself used to attend Holiness revivals. When young, I remember being extremely frightened of him and others speaking in tongues, shouting, and I remember being especially terrified of the phrase "baptism of fire." It sounded too much like Hell to me. And I was often afraid the Rapture would come and I'd be left with the sinners and the moon turned to blood. But I think I must have acquired some taste for the white-hot rhetoric of the New Testament, and for the ecstatic aspects of religion. I've always been moved by such ceremonies as the laying on of hands, foot washing, baptism.

But mostly I remember the great relief when the service was over, and we could go back out into the sunlight and the sweet breeze among the pines. There seemed a wonderful poise in nature, as it merely went about its business, with no interest or designs on us. How friendly the stars seemed over the dark mountains after the sweat of a prayer meeting. I have never enjoyed gatherings, whether lectures, classes, poetry readings. They seem to violate the essential and integral *aloneness* of poetry. Poetry at its best is the expression of the community, but through and to the solitary individual. In a similar way the doctrinal disputes I listened to as a child gave me a distaste for controversy and debate I've never been able to outgrow. Poetry does not argue; it affirms and embodies, or it is nothing.

SB: When you left Zirconia to go to college, you studied science, then math. What prompted the switch to English at Chapel Hill? Was it at this point that you knew you wanted to be a writer?

RM: All through my teens I wanted to be a writer. I had the example of Carl Sandburg just down the road in Flat Rock. A friend of mine had a brother at Harvard who sent us a paperback of *Crime and Punishment*. And there was a woman who drove the bookmobile who gave me *War and Peace* and Dickens. I read constantly, and I wanted to write. But I also wanted to be a composer, and studied piano, and books on harmony and technique, and banged on our old piano into the night, after working in the fields during the day. I wanted to be a philosopher also, and read Nietzsche, Sartre, Kant, Shaw, and anything I could get my hands on. Colin Wilson's *The Outsider* came out about that time, and I read that too, and thought about "existentialism."

I first went away to college at the age of sixteen, without graduating from high school, to Emory at Oxford, thinking of chemistry and medicine. But while there I got increasingly interested in calculus and the space program. John Glenn had just orbited the earth. At Emory I was at the top of my class in calculus, and I think it was vanity more than anything else that drove me toward mathematics. I was good, but not really that good. I made A's, but I would never have been a creative mathematician.

The year at NC State studying applied math and engineering was one of the most confused and exciting of my life. I found I could do my schoolwork in minimal time, so I really spent my days browsing in library and bookstore, walking in the city of Raleigh, going to the museum there, and to movies. I'd never been allowed to go to movies as a child, but I made up for it at college, attending every free flick, every foreign film, and every new release that came to Raleigh and Chapel Hill. I was so disturbed about what I wanted to do that I must have walked every block in the city of Raleigh. There was a lot of building going on then at NC State and in Raleigh, and the whole landscape seemed to be pits and heaps of red clay, new-poured cement, new expressways. I walked far into the suburbs and outskirts, stopping in diners and strange little restaurants. I was entirely on my own; I had no friends. One gray November afternoon I saw *Lolita* in a fleabag theater on the northwest side of the city, my first encounter with Nabokov.

In the spring of 1963 I wanted to take an advanced course in differential equations, but my adviser would not let me since I'd never made up a deficiency in solid geometry. So I registered for Creative Writing instead. The class was taught by Guy Owen, who was a generous and charming teacher. I wrote both poems and stories, but he encouraged the stories especially. The poems were terrible. I borrowed my roommate's typewriter and pecked away all spring, forgetting thermodynamics and partial differential equations, trying to remember exactly how my great aunts had spoken, and the smells of old houses heated by cooking stoves and fireplaces.

Even so, I wasn't ready to leave math entirely behind. When I transferred to UNC in 1963 I wanted to study both pure mathematics and comparative literature, if I remember correctly. So I took courses in Tolstoy and Dostoevsky as well as algebra and analysis. Chapel Hill seemed gentle and humane after the military atmosphere of NC State. I'll never forget how courteous everyone, from librarians to department secretaries, seemed. My two years as an undergraduate at Carolina were heady and invigorating. I met writers and actors, film makers and painters, worked on the *Carolina Quarterly,* saw hundreds of movies, studied the history of art, knew political activists and civil rights activists, beatniks who had lived in the East Village and Tangier. Around the *Quarterly* I got to know people with prep-school educations who knew far more about poetry than I. They talked about Yeats and Lowell and Berryman, and I began to listen.

I'd been writing poetry all along, but the first I did with any quality at all was in the late summer of 1964. I was working at the GE plant in Hendersonville, and looked out from the loading dock after a rain and saw a great shaft of sun coming through the overcast. I realized I wanted to describe that as a timber holding up and bracing the clouds. For days I wrote and rewrote, trying to get the verb and gesture of that image right. After returning to Chapel Hill I wrote a little piece inspired by Sibelius' "Swan of Tuonela." That was the first thing I ever did where I felt the sound was right. Guy Owen printed it in the *Southern Poetry Review* the next spring.

One of the finest things that happened to me at Chapel Hill was meeting Jessie Rehder, a wonderful teacher and encourager. It was she who invited me to work for Honors in writing, and to do that I had to become an English major. I abandoned math forever, though I'd finished most of the coursework for that degree, and wrote stories and poems, pieces of novels, film scripts and plays, during my senior year. In the fall of 1964, I felt that I too could write poetry, maybe, by being true to the world of experience beyond the ego, and true to the plainest, most honest voice. I heard a lucid, modern measure I wanted to learn to use, lean as Webern, subtle as Bartok, crisp as Pound's *Cathay*. I wrote scores of poems in 1964–65 trying to realize that voice. Mostly they didn't work out, but I felt privileged to be that close to something that seemed authentic.

SB: What's the relationship between your teaching and your writing? Do certain things change as an outgrowth of your teaching and research?

RM: Apparently my poetry began to change after I started teaching at Cornell. I'd lived so much in isolation, and worked at perfecting a compact kind of poem surrounded by silence, and rarely discussed writing with anyone except by letter. Suddenly I was working in a community where everyone seemed to be a writer, talking to dozens of students every day about their poetry. It was disorienting to say the least. But stimulating also, to find others interested in the same technical and poetic and historical questions I'd been working through.

My poems began to get more conversational, longer in wavelength and plot. As I taught and talked more, the poems began to talk more. But I didn't want to dilute the symbolic and emotional content for the sake of fluency. I've always been suspicious of the emphasis on "American speech" as any sort of artistic justification. The issue is poetic power, not manner. It was mostly this dilemma that almost brought my poetry writing to a halt in 1973, the year after *Red Owl* was published. I wanted concision and atomic density, but found I talked too easily. It was a dead end I didn't solve until a year later, when I began writing in rhymed forms. By focusing on end rhymes of the elaborate a b c c b a stanza or the chant royal I felt I'd recovered the necessary resistance for lines, and could go ahead. It was in that period that most of the *Land Diving* poems were written. That book means the most to me because in some ways it cost me the most. I found I was able to incorporate narratives and history, folktales and science, mono-logue and traditional forms into my writing, and that gave me a gratifying sense of control and freedom. I could write poems longer than a page, and integrate more levels of language and experience. I was no longer restricted to the tension of the free verse line I'd worked so hard to learn in the decade before. I tried writing a poem of over a hundred pages, from which I salvaged the fragments that later became *Trunk & Thicket*. It was just sheer good luck that a number of things came together for me around that time, from my reading of Smart's "Jubilate Agno," and discovering the rich textures of Geoffrey Hill's poetry, and beginning to fumble around with my own memories and childhood, with stories my grandfather and father had told, and a new coming to terms with the rhetoric of the New Testament, which I had forgotten since childhood. The poems of that period are probably uneven, but through them I found abilities I didn't know I had.

SB: In *Trunk & Thicket* you write about the instability and impotence of language. How do you reconcile this skepticism about language with your idealism and optimism about the function of poetry?

RM: In the passage you are referring to I mean my difficulties with speech more than with language itself. I have a light stammer, especially when excited or embarrassed. And I've always had a terror of having to *explain*. For every explaining seems to lead to yet another crux. There seems no end to formulation and argument. I often have an overwhelming sense of the futility of explaining anything. Only action matters. And poetry is action, is embodiment of idea and figure. Poetry is story, motion, not gloss or explication.

But I do have a skepticism about language too. It so rarely does what we want it to. The first step to becoming a writer is to learn to distrust words and the obvious combinations. You really have to hate the "poetic" effects to get anywhere as a poet. The more you know about language the more you see that it is all cliché, just a set of conventions. Every phrase wears out quickly. So you work against the erosion of freshness, that abrasion of use, not only by newness of diction and texture, but by voice and gesture. No word in itself is poetic for long, except by incorporating into the movement of voice, of imagination. It is not so much what is *said* as what is evoked, is enacted, by language that is important. A favorite quote is from Hollis Summers: "The point of a story is always the point beside the point." Peripheral vision is the important vision.

SB: Your cadence frequently resembles that of hymns. To what extent has music influenced the rhythm of your lines?

RM: Well, hymn meter is ballad meter, or common meter, which they say underlies all poetry in English. So in a sense it's hard to escape that sound in short poems, the four-stress line / three stress line. It must be in the very pulse of the language, like the two-stress hemistich of *Beowulf*, which one of my graduate students has found in Whitman.

Music has always been important to me. My mother sang to me often when I was little, and I used to make up long compositions in my head when I was a child, before I studied piano. It was as though everything I saw or thought had a musical correlative. But that fantasy stopped once I learned to read music. Later I wanted, more than anything, to be a composer.

But hymns may be just as important to me because of their words and imagery. They were certainly one of the art forms I was exposed to most as a child, along with readings from the Bible and the fine rhetoric of pulpit and prayer. I'm still haunted by the phrases of those lyrics: "There's a land that is fairer than day," "The land beyond the blue," "The river . . . that flows from the throne of God," "Beautiful, beautiful Zion," "By Jordan's stormy banks I'll stand."

SB: You've worked in areas virtually untouched by your contemporaries: anagrams, the complex French chant royal, and a stanza form Harmon calls the "morganelle." Would you discuss how you began to work with these and any such experiments in progress or planned?

RM: As I said earlier, I began working with traditional forms in 1974, after *Red Owl* was published. I'd tried some experiments, wedding the rich imagistic phrase with a more talky poem, and I'd not been happy with the results. Also, I was very busy teaching then, and almost quit writing for a while. But late in that year I suddenly began several projects at once. One was a series of poems on the ancient Near East, Sumer, and Akkad, which was never finished. Another was the long poem never finished but published in three fragments as *Trunk & Thicket*. The original idea was to write a long poem incorporating every verse form, from prose poem to free verse to blank verse to couplets right on through to triolets and rhyme royal. I saw the poem as a river gathering itself from many different-colored tributaries and passing through narrow gorges, over falls and shoals, through lakes and locks, and then unraveling itself through the delta and dispersing into the ocean. But I also tried to invent several new rhyme forms, including the one Harmon calls the "morganelle." I wanted to get a new cultural and historical richness and density in my work. At the same time I wanted to recover some of the incantatory power of "prophesying" as I'd heard it as a child. Suddenly I was able to confront and use that part of myself that had been rejected so long before. The result was "Mockingbird" and a pile of other poems I've never published but still plan to work on.

SB: To what extent is language a correlative of place in your poems? Does, then, a poem about a mountain carry with it the sense of stability, roughness, isolation that we associate with a mountain?

RM: This seems to be the area of poetics where contemporary literary theory has completely failed us. We seem to be living through a new age of nominalism in criticism. It's as though we have leapt back to the thirteenth century somehow. Theorists want to remind us that no word, no phrase, no sentence, has more than an arbitrary relationship with any fact, object, experience. In fact the only thing "real" about language is the structure and texture of language itself. But of course it is against the background of this very arbitrariness, this clutter, that any artist of language begins work. The fact that words are not written on gold in heaven in no way lessens their impact when put in the right order by a great poet. Poetry creates the *impression* of authority and plausibility; it delights and seems to be true to our experience.

As for a poem being like a mountain, nature is our only language for experience. If a poem is not to be big and grand and rough like a mountain, it would have to be big and rough as a bear, or wide as a river, or rough as the ocean in a gale, or long as the Milky Way. All description is metaphor, seeing and saying one thing as another. I wanted to write a poem big as the Cicero Mountain because that was the landform most familiar to me. I had grown up looking across the river valley at its woolly mammoth dome and long sloping shoulders, at the sparkling diamond eye where seepage froze on the cliff face in January. But image or fact in itself is never enough either. It is the equation of language with mountain (strange that it's named after old Cicero Ward, who was named after the orator). So mountain equals poem, grand, rough, isolate. The dirt and rocks and hollows of the mountains have not been changed in the least, and yet they have.

SB: What is your routine for writing? Do you set aside a certain amount of time each day?

RM: Poetry is so unpredictable you never know when you can start something, or if you do start it whether it will work out. Sometimes I've gone back through half-finished manuscripts and found one or two I could complete, often years after the first draft. At other times I've waited weeks for a new idea to come along. Poetry simply can't be written without enthusiasm for an image, a character, a tone of voice, that triggers a sense of possibility. Sometimes I don't have the confidence to write, and sometimes I wonder how I could have written what I have, much less something better, something different. You can't plan to write poetry, because the best things happen by surprise, while actually writing, while planning one kind of thing and finding that you've done another.

Hard as you may work on a poem, it's still a gift. A poem can't be worried into being, though it can certainly be revised and polished up. At the moment of writing, when things are coming together, you don't care much whether it's a great poem, or even a really good poem, as long as you can make it do what you have in mind, uncovering more and more possibilities. At the most intense times of composition you don't even care about "poetry" as long as you can make this one thing powerful in its own way. Literature is far from a working poet's mind.

SB: I haven't said much about your fiction, but I know you've written some short stories lately. What proportion of your writing time do you spend on that and how do you determine whether an idea is better suited to poetry or prose?

RM: Yes, I started writing stories again this summer for the first time in many years. I wrote a lot of fiction in college and started a couple of novels then, and actually published three or four stories, including one in the *Carolina Quarterly* way back. I've always been interested in fiction, and in fact have been working on a novel set in the sixties on a university campus in North Carolina (not any campus I was ever actually on, but a campus with elements of NC State maybe). It seemed like a very interesting setting for a novel.

I've always hated the overspecialization in American writing. Most people do either poetry or fiction, even specialize in a particular kind of poem or story or novel. I like to feel I have the freedom and ability to do both. I've also written some critical essays and reviews over the years. To some degree they all overlap. Certainly writing the poems has made me a better critic of poetry, and also a better prose stylist, a more accurate observer. But I had the experience when young of starting a story and becoming so interested in an image or a metaphor or rhythm I turned it into a poem. Gradually I wrote fewer and fewer stories and more and more poems. I was interested in compactness, and what I called "nonjournalis-tic" language. I hoped to find a new way of looking at the world around me. It seemed at the time that Faulkner and others had done the "southern fiction" idea to death. But there was almost no southern poetry. I wanted to work against the clichés of southern writing, and do something spare and precise, free of classical allusion and archaic diction. I found models in translations from Chinese poetry, and from the Greek anthology, and perhaps in laconic mountain speech.

Recently I have begun to take ideas that could become poems—but have not—and expand them into stories. That's the great difference be-tween stories and poems, besides the line unit; the story is much more detailed. In poems most details are left to implication.

SB: How do you know when a poem is finished?

RM: As someone else has said, they're never really finished, but aban-doned at some stage. But you do know when you can do no more with them. A line or image locks into place and you're willing to turn aside and work on something else in more need of revision.

SB: How do you explain the lack of critical attention you've received?

RM: I'm probably not the best person to answer that: I don't think there's been a lot of criticism of anybody of my generation. I've had a few very fine articles written on me: Harmon's is the longest, but there've been shorter ones from time to time. But I really think that my whole generation of poets has been neglected. The generation of poets born in the 1920s was so successful and so dominant that it has never been replaced, so that if anybody thinks of having a festival or writing an article, they think of somebody in the generation of Ashbery and Robert Bly and Gary Snyder, not of my generation. It's really just now that people in their late thirties and early forties are being taken all that seriously. That's a very compli-cated thing—the difference in generations. I think it has something to do with the fact that the older poets were the people who were in World War II and became writers after the war. It was a generation of great confidence and aggressiveness: they'd won the war. They believed in themselves and they took over. They were very critical of people older than them. I'm thinking about Ginsberg and Bly and Robert Creeley. Very critical of the New Critics—Allen Tate and people like that.

My generation, the Vietnam War generation, lost the war—lost the antiwar movement even—and have always been very confused about what they were up to and terribly polite to the older generation of poets. You never see an attack written by somebody my age on the generation of Ashbery and James Merrill. They always want to agree with them—very polite. And I think that's cost them tremendously. They haven't cleared any space for themselves. There are a few people who've had a little bit of critical attention, but very few. And this is not true of the older generation: by the time they were forty they'd been anthologized and written about.

Another reason for this is that my generation does not specialize in criticism, so that even the outstanding poets very rarely write articles on poetry. They are people who believe in the art of writing but not in developing critical approaches. The good side is I think my generation is just now beginning to come into its own. I think you'll see a change. It has taken a long time for us to really get going as writers. And I think that's true of other fields, not just poetry. But poetry, because it's the most essential art, reflects it the most dramatically.

SB: You've been labeled a "place poet," and a poet of "landscape"; William Harmon has called your poems "Pelagian georgics." Are you comfortable with these labels or do you feel they're too limiting? How would you categorize your poetry?

RM: I think all these terms apply in one way or another to what I've done. But you won't find many poets happy to categorize themselves. I think of myself as, hopefully, a poet, period. Certainly Harmon's phrase is the most unexpected, and the most resonant. He picked out the line in "Mockingbird" where I talk about the statute of limitations running out on original sin. That was said in fun, but I meant it too. I think that for me just becoming a writer, becoming a poet, necessitated a kind of distance from the fundamentalistic Baptist doctrine that I grew up with. It seemed so negative; it just cut off all possibility of creativity and growth. And I think this is true not only of me but of many American poets, going all the way back to Emerson and Thoreau and Whitman—coming out from under Calvinism and discovering something that worked better for them. The strange thing is that people like me repeat the process in the twentieth century. This has a lot to do with the place I come from and the world I grew up in. But even though I don't know where I stand theologically, I think Harmon is right that spiritually and emotionally I am a Pelagian. I have to believe in possibility, that there's not some great sin to be expiated but that there's a world there we can accept and appreciate, however doomed it may seem at times.

Why not try to work with what we have, what is here. As I say elsewhere, we are paradise's fools, surrounded by an Eden we can't even see. But the landscape I'm interested in is as much the landscape of language as the literal terrain. It has to work both ways to be interesting poetry. We live and speak in a landscape of symbols and references and cultural images and conditioning, as well as a world of trees and windy fields. Poems seem to explore the ways in which these things collide and contradict each other. If I felt older poetry adequately represented the world I've seen and imagined, there would be no need to write more. So you work partly out of a sense of failure, both your own and other poets'. If literature had said it all already I would just shut up and read and rake the yard. At the same time, you know that the odds are against you, even as you're driven to put more words on paper, to put all your money where your mouth is, and all the nerve you have, and then some. What a rebellious act it is for an American to even think of writing poetry. I'm still nervous about telling strangers I write. It's so much easier just to call yourself a teacher. That sounds okay; it doesn't embarrass anybody.

SB: What kinds of things can we expect to see from you after *Orchard Country?*

RM: That I really can't say. I have lots of ideas for poems, and forms I want to try, and half-finished poems I want to work again. And there's the stories, and the novel, and another book of poems that may be called *Detours*, but is a long way from completion. But I may never write another poem. It's just possible I've already had my say, and nothing new will surprise me into trying again. I hope not. For nothing else has pleased me quite as much. And it's possible that the best ideas and measures, ever, could be just waiting in the blue marrow of this pen.

The Rush of Language: Interview by
William Heyen and Stanley Rubin

Buffalo Trace

Sometimes in the winter mountains
after a little snow has blown in the night
and nothing's alive in eye-range
but the clouds
near peaks frozen clean
in the solstice sun,
the white finds a faint depression
to stick in out of wind
and makes visible for the first time
through woods and along the slopes
to where it nicks the rim
perceptibly, a ghostpath
under brush and broomsedge,
merging in the pasture with narrow
cowtrails but running on through fences
and across boundaries, under branches
in tattered sweep out to the low
gaps of the old migrations
where they browsed into the summer mountains
then ebbed back into the horizon
and back of the stars.

WH: I've liked the poem "Buffalo Trace" from the first time I read it. It begins with something close and then moves out, as so many of your poems do, through the collision of the buffalo and the cow all the way to the stars. I'm reminded of what you say in an essay: "The ear knows long before the mind whether a poem or passage is working." What about that idea regarding a poem like "Buffalo Trace?" I know Robert Frost said, "Watch my sentences." And I just have a feeling the way that poem works that it completed itself for you musically as much as it did intellectually or through idea.

RM: Poetry is in some ways a fairly primitive art. It belongs perhaps more to the Stone Age than to the twentieth century. It is primarily an art of sound. As Frost said, "The sound is the gold in the ore." I've noticed in writing and revising my own poems, and in reading the work of other poets including my students at Cornell, that I can tell whether a poem is going right first by the way it sounds; long before I figure out what's wrong with it, I can spot a weak passage because it doesn't sound right. Poetry is a miracle: it's the way we can say something that is true, that has depth, that has metaphoric resonance we don't always recognize at first, and we can say it in the fewest words possible—that's part of the poetic act also—and it's done somehow with the unconscious and the conscious working together. The sound is the testament of that; if it sounds right, it's probably saying the right things.

WH: Conciseness can actually lead to the poem's music.

RM: It can lead to the music and to new recognitions. Any number of times I've discovered in revising that I could take out a word or a short phrase and change the meaning slightly, and the new meaning would be better. It'd be a deeper poem with much greater ramifications. The art of poetry is to a great extent the art of compression and economy. Prose does not have to be so compact. Poetry is so much in the texture, in the sound, and that depends to a great extent on how quickly something is being said. As I say in my essay in your anthology, the music of poetry, especially modern poetry, is derived as much from that compression and concision as it is from the stresses. You can, after all, write something very dull in iambic pentameter. Our sense of the music is some strange fusion of the content and the quickness of the expression, with the stresses, the syllables.

SR: You see the music, then, as being the connection with the primitive.

RM: Right. It's something of the ear and of the senses, of the body as much as of the mind. I can see that especially in a poet like Eliot, whom I was teaching yesterday. Even if you don't understand "Prufrock"—and I'm not sure I understand it although I've been reading it for twenty-five years—you're still haunted by the music of it. It's like Mozart; once you've heard it, you never forget it.

Another test of poetry is memorability; that is, if you want to say it aloud, to repeat it, then it's probably good poetry.

SR: Does this argue in some way for the traditional approach to music and meter in poetry?

RM: It's very hard to get away from them. Those traditional devices of poetry were discovered and used for a good reason—they worked, they delighted the ear.

That's one reason poetry has lost its large audience. I don't think the general public has ever taken to free verse; free verse sounds like poetry to poets and literary people, but when the average person thinks of poetry, he or she thinks of Poe, who is in some ways our poet laureate. If you ask people to repeat a line of Whitman, they probably can't do it; but if you ask them to repeat a line of Poe, everybody can say, "Once upon a midnight dreary, while I pondered, weak and weary." Those trochees just trip off in their minds.

WH: And there's been a flattening in general in contemporary poetry, I think, and it's ironic that much of the flattening is the result of poets trying to reach an audience; but, as you've said, plain speech sounds like poetry only to poets.

RM: People delight in music, and they get that kind of poetry these days from rock 'n' roll and folk songs and country music. There's a lot of poetry all around us. Poetry is not just verse; it's not just T. S. Eliot. Poetry is any imaginative use of language, of metaphor and figure: it's in prose, it's in fiction, it's in editorials. Often we feel it's not as sophisticated as the poetry we try to write.

WH: How did you get started? Where did poetry enter your life?

RM: The traditional answer for a southern writer is to say, "Of course, I absorbed poetry from the oral tradition in the South," and that's partly true in my case. I heard a lot of storytelling around the fireplace; I grew up in a community that was still in some ways in the nineteenth century, and people talked more than they do now. They told stories, and southerners *are* particularly good storytellers.

The other answer for a southern writer is, "I got it from the King James version of the Bible and from preachers." There is *that* oral tradition in the South, and that's certainly true in my case. I heard a lot of great preaching, and I grew up in a very religious family—we read the Bible twice a day, prayed three or four times a day—so I was exposed to that very rich Elizabethan rhetoric of the New Testament.

The first time I read modern poetry was when I was about fifteen, and my sister had gone off to Bob Jones University, where she used Cleanth Brooks's anthology of American literature in freshman English. She brought it home one weekend, and in paging through it I came upon Whitman. I remember vividly reading the first lines of "Song of Myself": "I celebrate myself, and sing myself, / And what I assume you shall assume, / For every atom belonging to me as good belongs to you." But the lines that really leapt out at me were "I loafe and invite my soul, / I lean and loafe at my ease observing a spear of summer grass." It was the contrast between "soul" and that one "spear of grass" that really struck me. I thought, My goodness, you can go from something that grand to something that precise and small. It was that juxtaposition that first started me thinking about poetry, and, of course, that's exactly the way poetry works— in the positioning of the big with the little, making the far near, and the near far.

At the same time, in flipping further, I came upon Wallace Stevens, whom I'd never heard of. I read "Domination of Black," where he talks about how the leaves turn, as the fire turned, and he looks out the window and sees the planets turn—that correspondence between the things very close and very far—and I never forgot that. I didn't know anything about poetry, never read Stevens or Whitman again for years, but I never forgot that. It seemed to have planted a seed of some sort.

It's also true that living just down the road in Flat Rock was Carl Sandburg, who had bought an antebellum mansion there. He was always in the paper—he was going to Hollywood or New York—so I had a model of somebody who was a professional poet.

SR: You mentioned Sandburg, and so much of your early work is concerned with the western Carolina mountains and the country you spent your boyhood in. Some of that poetry is suggestive of Sandburg. I wonder if you would say more about the influence of your region and your boyhood on your work.

RM: The irony is that Sandburg, of course, has been associated with the Midwest. It was only after World War II that he moved to North Carolina. But I did admire his work, and it gave me ideas about poetry—its vernacularity or conversational tone—a poetry aimed at ordinary people. He said that he wanted to write for the truck driver and the waitress, and that was certainly one of my ideas early in my writing.

I think he's a very underestimated poet, actually; he's forgotten, partly as poetry has moved deeper and deeper into the academy to become something for a graduate seminar. Sandburg needs little explication; therefore, he's not read much. Stevens would be the perfect poet for the graduate seminar because he's so "difficult." Difficulty has become a measure of quality.

But I didn't really think of myself as a writer about the southern mountains until I came up north. I had written some about it, but I really thought of myself as an American poet. The models I had in mind at that time were Sandburg and Gary Snyder and Robert Bly, the great influences on me in my early twenties. But I did begin to discover that I had a subject.

I decided about 1965 or 1966 that I wasn't going to write fiction for a while—I had written stories and even published a few—because southern fiction had been "done." It was what we associated with the South and southern writing—Faulkner, Eudora Welty, Walker Percy—but there was no such thing as "southern poetry," and certainly very little poetry about the southern mountains. That seemed an opportunity.

I decided consciously to do something different from what was thought of as traditional southern writing—which was very colorful and highly rhetorical. I wanted to become a writer of very precise poems, concise poems. The models in American literature I found the most useful were Thoreau and, to some extent, Dickinson. As I say in my essay in *The Generation of 2000*, I wanted an almost classical concision and precision with no rhetoric, or very few rhetorical effects. I wanted something very direct, honest. The models I found that I admired most then were Thoreau's poems in *Walden*—the "Smoke" poem, the "Haze" poem—and at that time I would take the simplest and most ordinary thing and try to write a poem, about gravity or copper or a chair. I was taking Whitman literally, when he said: "If you want me again look for me under your boot soles." He's speaking as the spirit of American poetry—not literally as Walt Whitman, but as the American imagination. And he was right: you find the poetry wherever you are, just looking in the most unexpected places. You don't need anything grand as the subject of a poem. You find the grandeur within the poem as you write it.

WH: Would you talk about and maybe read "Mountain Bride?"

RM: After I came to Cornell, I began to get interested in two or three things that were new for me. One was writing in traditional forms, like the ballad; another was writing narrative poetry; and a third was writing some of the stories that had been told to me by my grandfather and other people—to get the folklore or the legend of a place into poetry. This is an example of one of the poems I wrote back then.

It's called "Mountain Bride." This is a story told to me by the fireplace by my grandfather when I was a kid. Scared me to death, as many of these stories did! I later found out that it is a traditional Appalachian folktale. He told it as though it had happened just up the road; of course, that's the way folktales should be told.

Mountain Bride

They say Revis found a flatrock
on the ridge just
perfect for a natural hearth,
and built his cabin with a stick

and clay chimney right over it.
On their wedding night he lit
the fireplace to dry away the mountain
chill of late spring, and flung on

applewood to dye
the room with molten color while
he and Martha that was a Parrish
warmed the sheets between the tick

stuffed with leaves and its feather
cover. Under that wide hearth
a nest of rattlers,
they'll knot a hundred together,

had wintered and were coming awake.
The warming rock
flushed them out early.
It was she

who wakened to their singing near
the embers and roused him to go look.
Before he reached the fire
more than a dozen struck

and he died yelling her to stay
on the big four-poster.
Her uncle coming up the hollow
with a gift bearham two days later

found her shivering there
marooned above a pool
of hungry snakes
and the body beginning to swell.

WH: I like that poem. In Pound's sense, it's "news that stays news," because even though I know what's going to happen, I keep enjoying the reading of it.

You said once that you thought a poem is the closest thing you know to a perpetual motion machine. What did you mean by that?

RM: The poem is a verbal machine—that's Williams' definition—I like that sense of objectivism, the poem as an object. A really good poem seems to renew itself with every generation, with every reader, and I'm not sure exactly how this happens, but it's the miracle of poetry that it does. Somebody can write a "Lycidas" or the seventy-third sonnet of Shakespeare that seems to have an energy of its own but also a power to transform the future into new energy. Long after the writer's gone with whatever energy he put into it, the poem keeps renewing itself.

WH: It keeps moving with that vertical audience down through time. I like that.

RM: It's also able somehow to assimilate the energy of whatever age it's read in, using new concepts to renew itself. Dante's a good example. No matter what happens in astronomy or psychology, Dante seems to have already been there. His image of the universe is perfectly consonant with relativity, quantum mechanics, the newest discoveries in astronomy, the notion of a circular universe. I think the reason is that the imagination is universal, and no matter where human beings look they will come up with essentially the same metaphors. As far as I'm concerned, science is just as imaginative as poetry: it's all part of the same imagination looking for metaphors and a vocabulary for explaining experience.

WH: And Shakespeare knew everything that Jung was to discover.

RM: Everything there is to know has already been known; we just keep inventing new figures of speech for it.

SR: Clearly you don't believe in this split between science and poetry that has been made much of in our century by Christopher Clausen and others. On the other hand, you are an exception as a poet, in having had training in science.

RM: I've found that most poets have an interest in science. Science is in a way the theology of the twentieth century; it's important to us in the way that mystic philosophy and theology were to Dante. That was for Dante the new explanation of reality. Insofar as we have an authoritative new theology in our century, it is Einstein's and Darwin's. Insofar as we believe in truth, it's there.

Of course, this is a great issue for modern poetry: what is truth? We are no longer as confident of the Romantic answers as people like Emerson and Whitman were. They said, "Look into the self, and whatever seems true to yourself is truth." One of the great issues for us has been, What is the self? Is there a self? Can we know the self?

Eliot's answer was that truth comes from the tradition: you cannot know it on your own; you have to learn it from society, from the community. Truth is a communal act. That's true particularly for poetry and language, because language is a communal instrument. It's not something you would arrive at on your own. This has been proven. Somebody who lives in isolation doesn't develop very much in the use of language. Poetry is a thing of the community.

WH: You read a poem last night that held your audience—it's called "The Gift of Tongues." It goes back to the religious experience of your childhood, and it talks about language in some of the ways you've been talking about.

RM: As I said earlier, I was raised in a very religious household. My mother was a Southern Baptist, and my father was a Pentecostal Holiness; and I went to both kinds of services. At one service that I remember going to, my father spoke in tongues. I had heard other people speak in tongues, but it seemed different when he did it. It was terrifying!

The Gift of Tongues

The whole church got hot and vivid
with the rush of unhuman chatter
above the congregation,
and I saw my father looking at
the altar as though electrocuted.
It was a voice I'd never heard
but knew as from other centuries.
It was the voice of awful fire.
"What's he saying?" Ronald hissed
and jabbed my arm. "Probably Hebrew."
The preacher called out another
hymn, and the glissade came again,
high syllables not from my father's
lips but elsewhere, the flare of
higher language, sentences of light.
And we sang and sang again, but
no one rose as if from sleep to
be interpreter, explain the writing
on the air that still shone there like
blindness. None volunteered a gloss
or translation or receiver
of the message. My hands hurt
when pulled from the pew's varnish
they'd gripped and sweated so. Later,
standing under the high and plain-
sung pines on the mountain I clenched
my jaws like pliers, holding in
and savoring the gift of silence.

As I said last night, I think I've finally figured out what the poem is about. What was so frightening was the sense of language being used under inspiration but without control. It's important for poets to feel a sense of control at the same time they are inspired. You have the rush of language, but you're in control of it. It's conscious mind and the unconscious working together. So much of the power of poetry comes from that particular fusion of unconscious, memory, dream, with consciousness. It's that place or threshold that people in the nineteenth century called "reverie," the place where there's an intermingling, a washing back and forth between dream, sleep, and consciousness. It takes both the control of consciousness and the rush from the unconscious to write good poetry. Poets are people sensitive to that particular threshold; they can put themselves into that state of semipassivity.

After I got to college, I looked up books and articles on speaking in tongues, or glossolalia, and I found out in psychological studies that it's related to epilepsy and hypnosis. Certain cells in the brain fire off when triggered by eye contact from a charismatic leader. It's a very primitive, ancient kind of thing, and it was always seen as a visitation of some sort, back into the Stone Age. Remember that in earliest recorded history epileptics were considered gifted people, inhabited by good demons.

SR: This is a very rich area you've opened up here. One is the issue of control. You're suggesting that this kind of energy and power is close to what the poet feels, but without the control it isn't poetry.

RM: My favorite line in all of Emerson's poetry is in his poem "Bacchus," the Dionysian poem of the pair, "Merlin" and "Bacchus"— "Merlin" is wisdom; "Bacchus," drunkenness. Of course, he means drunkenness in the spiritual sense; he talks about the wine that doesn't come from the grape. He says that in that state of blessed drunkenness or intoxication, he'll "hear far Chaos talk with me." That's it! You're close enough to hear chaos, but you're not in it. If you were *in* chaos, you couldn't write it; it'd be pure turbulence. Poets are people who can get close enough to chaos to feel the rush of energy, that primordial power of the imagination, but they can control it within a form.

SR: They are not just the vehicles or mediums for it; they have the requirement of craft and, as you're suggesting, conscious awareness of tradition.

RM: They're makers, craftsmen or craftswomen, as well as mediums.

SR: In a related area, I'd like to ask you about your language. The poem you just read, which is recent, uses terms like glissade and phrases like "sentences of light," which are by no means vernacular; yet you, like so many contemporary poets, come out of that tradition of being in touch with the vernacular. It's very clear that you transform American speech, that you won't render just the looseness of overheard speech. I wonder if there is a tension or even a paradox somewhere at the heart of American poetry that we must all contend with: namely, fulfilling that commitment to being vernacular, populist, and yet maintain a special obligation to language. Have I said too much?

RM: No, I'm very concerned with that, and I've never settled that issue for myself. I'm beginning to suspect that vernacularity in poetry is one of the myths of Romanticism we love. We want to give the impression that we are writing in the vernacular.

The man who articulated this theory was Wordsworth, and he was never able to live up to the theory. The next man to articulate it was Whitman, and if you know Whitman, you know that whatever he's doing it's not the vernacular, the spoken language of America. It's very elevated language that gives the impression of an oratorio, or an Italian bel canto opera.

It's a part of our democratic heritage: we want to believe that everything we do is for everybody. But sophisticated poetry, in fact, is probably not going to be read by everybody.

There's a long, painful history for me in that. I started out wanting to write for everybody, and I've gradually come to realize that really good poets probably don't. You're writing for people who are pretty literate. In that sense, I am not a "folk poet," even though I've been called one. You use words like glissade, and it shows you know something about ballet. It's based on a cultural tradition, as well as a folk tradition. I don't think it's important, finally, what kind of language you use as long as you accomplish aesthetically what you want to in a poem. A theory of poetry is much less important than the poem itself.

In fact, what really good American writers do is give a plausible impression of vernacularity. Look at Hemingway's dialogue, which seems realistic, but, of course, it's not. It's highly compressed. We want to give that impression because we are the inheritors of that myth of the common man and the myth that poetry is common speech. Even somebody like Sandburg who tried hard to write ordinary speech did it only in bits and pieces, gists of slang here and there to give the impression. The local color writers of the turn of the century experimented with this, and they're mostly bad writers because they were trying to be true to the native speech of Maine or Georgia more than the art of storytelling; they rendered the speech but they didn't write very good stories or poems for the most part.

SR: As teachers we've all encountered the motivation students have sometimes in starting this business of poetry—wanting to be prophet figures, or to have that connection to the mass they don't otherwise feel. That often seems to come from this wrong image of Whitman we've perpetuated—that he wandered around, speaking the speech of common people and naming everything, and that's all they have to do to become poets.

RM: He wanted to give that impression; that was part of his legend.

SR: Maybe because poetry has lacked a clear place in our culture from the beginning, American poets have been particularly afraid of the isolation and loneliness and inwardness that poetry comes out of and they have been particularly defensive, proclaiming our poetry gets its justification from its important themes and cultural statements. But in actuality poetry comes out of language. Maybe we need to acknowledge that we are in some sense unwillingly an elite, or at least a minority, in responding to language in that way.

RM: The other danger in that area is going too far toward specialization in vocabulary. In academia this is particularly a problem of a priestcraft evolving a jargon for ourselves that nobody else understands. You see that priestcraft particularly in critics who have a magic language, and graduate students who come to them to learn it.

I'm not interested in being that specialized. I would like to see poetry achieve a classic balance between sophistication and precision, in a vocabulary that can say with great subtlety exactly what you want to say. I would not like to go to either extreme—poems that anybody can understand on the first hearing or poems that are completely hermetic.

SR: You are not, I gather, particularly enamored of Ashbery's work.

RM: He interests me a great deal—especially before he was canonized as the great romantic poet. Back in the sixties I read his dada poems; they're a lot of fun. But he doesn't interest me as much as somebody like Geoffrey Hill or T. S. Eliot, somebody whose difficulty is part of the complexity of what he's trying to say. It's not difficulty for the sake of difficulty.

I have a recent poem that deals with my interest in language. I'd like to read "Writing Spider."

Writing Spider

When Uncle Wass had found the spider's
W woven between the limbs
of a dead chestnut over on
the Squirrel Hill, he said he knew
there would be war. But even before
Pearl Harbor he was gone himself
and my Grandpa, his brother, told
how the writing spider's runes could spell
a message to the world, or warn
of the individual reader's own
end with an initial. That web
was strung significant as lines
in a palm and the little webster,
spinning out its monogram like
the fates, put the whole dictionary
of a life in one elaborate
letter to be abstracted from
the Jacob's ladder of floss and dew
in the eye of the beholder,
a lifetime's work for it and all.

This poem is related to an idea I keep going back to—the way we find writing in nature. Science is really doing that. It's decoding one kind of writing everywhere it looks. Everything is language.

WH: What about in the suburbs, "at the edge of the orchard country?" Where, then, is the nature?

RM: That's one of the problems for contemporary, and perhaps future, American poets. American poetry starts with Emerson, whose first book is called *Nature*. Our first poets evolved a tradition of celebrating nature and reading nature as a mirror of the self, as an image or a language of the soul.

The best clue to what can be done in the suburbs is probably William Carlos Williams. There's someone who confronted this issue way back in the twenties.

The problem is that the suburbs are a world in between. There's great poetry of the city, in Whitman and Hart Crane, Ginsberg, and great poetry of nature. How do you make a poetry of the middle landscape, the middle range of experience, the bedroom towns? No one has done that very well, except Williams. It violates the grain of American poetry.

Conversation with William Harmon

1990

WH: I've been conversing with Robert Morgan for going on twenty years now, but not out loud or necessarily in public, as far as I know, so let me just invite you all to join the two of us in a conversation that began years ago and will continue for many more years, I hope. Recently, the things that we have been talking about are Buicks, including Karl Shapiro's poem called "Buick," and the perfidy and fecklessness of all publishers, among other topics. I brought almost all of Bob's books along. I've got a copy of *Zirconia Poems*, the first book, which is out of stock, also the great volume *Trunk & Thicket*, which is also no longer for sale. Most of the others seem to be available. Let me invite you to take part in the conversation actively, please.

Yesterday, a couple of the people were asking how it is that a writer who is from this place and writes of this place doesn't really live in this place. There was a kind of question there about what you write about and where you truly dwell. One of the best writers living in the South has lived in the region for nearly fifty years but is not a southern writer—Laura Riding Jackson, whom I saw about two weeks ago. She is nearly ninety and lives in Wabasso, Florida, but is in no way southern at all. Meanwhile, quite a few southern writers—undeniably southern—have lived in Connecticut, Minnesota, England, and all kinds of remote places and seem to do all right. I thought we would start by talking about that. I'm from North Carolina and I live about one hundred miles from where I was born. I've got to for dietary reasons. I can't be too far from a certain style of barbecue. I confess I've driven one hundred miles for lunch. I don't think I could live away from North Carolina. I've tried it for fourteen years in various places, but it didn't work. I had to come back. How do you do it? How do you stay away?

RM: Cornell offered me a job in 1971. I was unemployed except when I could pick up house-painting jobs at $2.00 an hour in Henderson County. Cornell paid a little bit more and the work was steadier. But I went up north for one year—they gave me a job for one academic year and I expected to be back in Henderson County at the end of that year. Somebody else went on leave the next year at Cornell and they invited me to stay for 1972–1973. In the spring of 1973 the department chairman called me into his office, and I thought he was going to say, There's nothing left for you; instead he said, Would you like to be a professor here? And in a perhaps weak moment I said, yes, I would stay on. I think it never really occurred to me that I was a southern writer and an Appalachian writer until I left the region. To tell you the truth, when I was writing the early poems, the poems in *Red Owl*, I kind of thought of myself in the company of Baudelaire in Paris and Pasternak in Moscow and Gary Snyder in Berkeley. I had not thought that much about the region. It was only after I had left it that I got increasingly interested in the history and geography and geology of the southern mountains. And I'm not sure I would have ever written as much about the place if I had stayed down here. I can't know that, but because I was away from it I was awfully nostalgic and began to think more and more about it. I still do; particularly in the wintertime up north I just ache to be back in the South and see that sunshine on the south slopes and this time of year to see the trees budding out. I miss the speech, the accent. This is not to say I don't like it in upstate New York. I do like it at Cornell.

WH: I believe you said to me once that this title, *At the Edge of the Orchard Country*, is true of Henderson County, but it's also true of where you live in New York.

RM: Tompkins County, New York.

WH: It's also orchard country, though it may not be that daily.

RM: It turns out that upstate New York, which is where I live, is part of Appalachia—a northern extension, and during the war-on-poverty years, it was considered a part of Appalachia. If you get away from Ithaca and away from Cornell, some of the hollows look very much like western North Carolina, even down to the old cars sitting out in front of the houses, and bathtubs with flowers in them. There are so many examples of writers who have written about a place they're living away from. The best example is Joyce, who left Dublin when he was twenty-two, I believe, and never lived there again. He moved to Paris and then Trieste and to Zurich and Paris again. Everything he wrote is about Ireland, about Dublin. They say you can reconstruct a map of Dublin circa 1904 from *Ulysses*. A lot of

American writers of course went to Paris in the twenties—Gertrude Stein lived in Paris all of her life after she left medical school at Johns Hopkins, and most of her writing is about America in one way or another, even about the American language. Pound lived away from America most of his life and was obsessed with American vernacular and, as you know, American history and economics, and he knew a lot more about the Revolutionary period and Federalist period than most of us.

WH: I read a thing once about Hilda Doolittle, known as H.D., who lived most of her adult life in Europe after growing up in Pennsylvania; and somebody speculated that, if your language is the stuff of daily life for you, then it's not a very good aesthetic medium. The aesthetic medium needs to be a little bit removed from the commerce and so forth, but if you were away from home, exiled some way, and the language that you had to use for daily life was French, say, or German—even British English—then this frees up your native dialect to be an aesthetic medium and also do the same kind of aestheticizing to your native landscape and people, and so forth. So it may be that one way at least is to leave home, and it then permits your home materials to become aesthetic more easily; but some writers have stayed right where they were born and have done all right. They have had to be creative.

RM: There are not many writers who have stayed always within their region. Hardy could be used as an example of somebody who stayed in Dorset and wrote about Dorset all his life. Though in fact he started writing, I think, when he was living in London as an architect.

WH: He may be like Faulkner, to and from New Orleans, eventually back home again. I was going to ask you about Hardy because, like Hardy, you have now combined writing prose fiction with poetry. Even like Hardy you began as a fiction writer and the poetry came afterwards, and now you've gone back to fiction. . . . Robert Creeley said that he began as a writer in the forties and regarded himself as a writer of prose fiction—and the poetry only came later. It baffles me that this can be done. I could not write fiction. I've never done it. I began writing a short story one time and I wrote the first clause; I wrote, "It had been in all the papers." Then I went back and said, "It had been in all of the papers." Then I said, "It had been in all the newspapers." Then I said, "It had been in all of the newspapers." See the poet's bad habit of squeezing every word. Then I saw I never could do it. And I had no voice to speak in and no medium, so I left. It's a pretty good story so far and I'll finish it maybe some decade soon, but I've had the wrong habits for it. Two things about Hardy: one is that he achieved something like a level of genius in both fiction and poetry, and that he did them in the wrong order. He did the fiction first. He wrote 14 novels and maybe 50 stories and then wrote most of his poems after age fifty-eight. He didn't know that he had thirty more years to live, but he really had two consecutive thirty-year careers, the first in fiction, the second in poetry. That is really astonishing. What interests me—is the prose written by somebody who is a poet different from other people's prose? It's an interesting question. I didn't notice in *The Blue Valleys* that your prose, as such, is poetical.

RM: Well, it's a well-known pitfall to poets who write fiction that they try to write fancy poetic prose and I tried to make clean-cut prose. I think writing poetry helps me as a prose writer, with the economy of language.

WH: Are you still working on that novel you said you were writing?

RM: I'm still working on it. I started a novel in 1980 and worked on it for a year and put it aside, and went back to it in the mid-eighties and have gone back to it again recently. I find it very difficult to write. I think short stories and poems are much closer than short stories are to novels. The difficult thing about the novel is it's so big and there are so many characters and you've got to keep so many things going on simultaneously. It's just plain hard work, but most people know that. Poets lack the navigational skills for novel writing.

WH: But you're still working on it, right?

RM: I hope to finish it in the next year or two.

WH: I'll ask people about a number of writers like Kipling and George Meredith who could be both poetry and fiction writers. Fairly often there is a very distinct discrepancy. Is there a doctrine about this? Why is Hardy by himself? Or is he?

RM: No, he's not. D. H. Lawrence is almost equally ambidextrous. Lawrence has such a powerful voice that it comes through in whatever he writes. Melville is certainly a better novelist, but he wrote very, very good poems. And Dylan Thomas. William Carlos Williams' best writing, I think, is in his short stories. There's a tendency in American culture, or perhaps modern culture, to be specialized. You become an electrical engi-

neer, you become a television electrical engineer—you work in one part
of the television technology. I think it is more interesting for writers to deal
in many literary forms. I find it refreshing when I reach an impasse in
poetry and can turn back to fiction writing or vice versa. I have gotten
ideas from writing poetry that I have used in fiction and vice versa.

WH: Philip Larkin said once that something was either a short short
story or a novel. To him, the idea of a long poem was uncongenial. Anybody want to join in?

Q: Have you started any poems that then turned into fiction or vice
versa?

RM: Not recently, but back in the sixties, when I switched increasingly
to poetry, that happened. I would have an idea and start working on it and
get intrigued by association or a metaphor and it would turn into a poem.
That doesn't happen so much now. I have an idea for a story and I usually
pursue it. One of the things you learn to do when you practice writing a
lot is to try to finish whatever you start, at least in a draft. It's very helpful
to do that—not to give up midway. Often something that seems unprom-
ising midway will turn out to be pretty good. You never know. I used to
work with my dad, who is a house painter as well as a farmer, and he
would tell me no matter how bad things are going in the morning they will
probably get better—just keep going. And he was right. I do get ideas for
poems in the process of writing stories. When they come to mind, I jot
them down in my notebook and come back to them.

Q: Do you think that it is true, and why, if it is true, that people who
write about New York City are "writers" and people who write about the
Appalachian Mountains are "regional writers?"

WH: I once heard John Hollander describe himself as a "New York
hick."

RM: There's a tendency of a dominant culture to look upon the other
parts of the kingdom or the country as regional perhaps. But it also works
the other way. People who are at what is perceived as the center of the
culture are often fascinated by people from the outlands. In the British
Isles, this is true of Ireland, say. They've admired Irish writers even though
they might have treated Ireland shabbily; and the British theater, and to
some extent poetry and fiction, have been Irish for a hundred years or so.
You can see this in American culture, both in the fascination with the

southern fiction of the twentieth century and with Hollywood's obsession with the South and the Civil War. The first great American movie was *The Birth of a Nation*, the most famous movie of all time is *Gone with the Wind*. It's a pattern that's repeated in history many times: the Normans conquer England in the eleventh century and become obsessed with the Celtic past of Britain and create the Arthurian and Grail literature and pass this on to the Continent. Southern writers have a kind of advantage there, and perhaps in the future Appalachian writers may seem important because they are from a different place. That "difference" is useful.

WH: We've discussed this before, but I remember as a kid in North Carolina I made two discoveries: I lived in the same place as *Gone with the Wind*, and I lived in the same place as Li'l Abner. I was not the aristocracy of the columned mansion, nor could I identify with the picturesque peasantry of Al Capp or Erskine Caldwell. I was surprised to find out that this was the same region Concord, North Carolina, was in. I couldn't recognize that accent, as you say. This was a shock to me, and I was also surprised to find out that we had lost the war; they had not told me, you know. "The War"—there was only one war back then. There was another war in Europe at the time, but we used to have May 10 as Confederate Memorial Day in North Carolina in my childhood. We put flowers on the monument and sang "The Bonny Blue Flag." If anybody mentioned that the South was on the losing side, I wouldn't believe it. I'll tell you a story about my hometown. There used to be a house on Union Street in Concord where Jefferson Davis had spent the night after the war had ended. The old sign said, "Jefferson Davis, President of the Confederacy, fleeing south after Lee's surrender, spent the night of April 18, 1865, in this house." Then the house was torn down and the sign was also taken away, and later a sign reappeared with many more spaces, just as a computer justifies the right margins, and said, "Jefferson Davis, President of the Confederacy, spent the night of April 18, 1865, in a house near here." They had left out that nonsense about fleeing south after Lee's surrender. That "southernness" that we find in various movies and cartoons and other media was not immediately something I identified with as a southern child. I grew up in the specific South of a cotton-mill town. Nunnally Johnson is a writer from Savannah, Georgia, and somebody asked him in the thirties if he thought Erskine Caldwell drew an accurate picture of life in that part of Georgia, and Johnson said, "Oh my Lord, yes, those up country people are just terrible snobs."

RM: In 1967 or '68, I started writing about things that I had never seen poems about, like hog pens and manure piles. And people would come up to me and say, "You're so lucky you have all this wonderful material to write about." And at that time I felt disadvantaged that I didn't go to Harvard like John Ashbery and I didn't live in Paris or London. It turns out that you can write about anything.

WH: *You* can. I think you have us all beat. You write a poem about an odometer or a glove compartment, but I think it's *Sigodlin* that has a poem that is the extreme of writing a poem about something that nobody else would ever think of writing a poem about. It's called "Stretching." It's a wonderful poem. It never occurred to me to write a poem about stretching, even though this is exactly something that I go through forty or fifty times a day.

I've written down a couple of other things I wanted to ask you about— your notebook, for instance. That interests me. I don't have one. I can't remember what I write down so it doesn't make any sense to me to say something like "coat hanger." Do I buy a coat hanger or do I write about one, or what? I'm like McGyver, the unarmed policeman. I exist that way. Maybe I should do something different, but I'm too old to change. What are your notebooks like?

RM: Well, they change. They used to be a lot better than they are now. Back in the sixties and seventies, I kept notebooks and would write out paragraphs about poetics, and history, or quotations I thought were impressive, ideas for poems, or even a few lines of a poem. I don't know what happened, but in the late seventies, my notebooks got thinner and thinner—words, maybe a phrase, an idea, something that I had read in a history book that I thought might make an interesting poem, odd facts. In 1975 I typed up notes from several notebooks for Danny Marion's special issue of *The Small Farm*. Back then I had real notebooks. But once I started writing more essays and working on fiction, I spent less time on the notebooks.

WH: They used to tell us in school to hand in our notes and outline. Everybody I knew did the outline after they had written the paper. How do you know what you're going to say until you see what you've done? I never could take notes.

RM: All fiction writers keep notebooks to write down ideas for stories, the characters, their relationships, or a plot idea. Even though you don't use most of them, it is something you can go back to if you need an idea.

WH: What's the farthest you ever went in a poem toward chaos?

RM: Oh, passages in *Trunk & Thicket*. I was trying to write incantatory poetry. In 1974 I got very interested in writing a totally different kind of poetry. Among other things, I went back and started reading the Bible for the first time since my teens. And I also read Christopher Smart's great poem "Jubilate Agno"—"Rejoice in the Lamb"—which is a wonderful incantatory poem. And for several months I wrote in a style unlike anything I had ever done before, or since. I think I was a little mad. It was a style I plan to return to sometime. You once wrote an essay called "Robert Morgan's Pelagian Georgics" and took the line from *Trunk & Thicket* that said the statute of limitations had run out on original sin as your theme. The heresy that denies original sin was originated by the theologian Pelagius. He was a Briton, and his name back in Britain was Morgan. *Morgan* in Welsh means "of the sea" or "by the sea," and *Pelagius* is *Morgan* translated into Greek.

Q: I grew up in the mountains of North Carolina. I detect a remarkable loss of local color in language. If this is so, how will it affect our literature?

RM: I think it is why so many people are writing about the area. As you lose something, it becomes more important and it also becomes available for writing. At the end of the Puritan era, people like Hawthorne could write about it. It's very hard to write about something while it's going on—you can't see it while it's around you. I think I, and a lot of other people, are writing about the mountain past because we feel we are very quickly losing it and we want to recapture it. Once I gave a reading in Hendersonville and one of my cousins, I think the only relative of mine who has ever come to a poetry reading, came to me and said: "It's wonderful. You can actually remember how it was. I had forgotten those things." I think that's an important function of writing.

Q: New generations will not have this understanding?

RM: Except in writing, perhaps.

Q: What makes "things Appalachian" appeal on the outside, at a national level, like Cormac McCarthy does? Much of the writing is nostalgic and pastoral. Do you consider yourself an Appalachian writer?

RM: They tell me that when I came up for tenure at Cornell one of my colleagues said: "Well, he doesn't write about anything except North Carolina. Why should we give him tenure and keep him here?" And other colleagues obviously disagreed with that. I think you're absolutely right that the kind of writing that tends to be popular in any time and from any area is the kind that answers stereotypes. And Hollywood and pop culture have taught America what to look for in the South and in the mountains. If you conform to those stereotypes it is easier to be popular, because people like things they are accustomed to. They like to go to horror movies because they like to be scared, but scared by something they know is going to be over soon and fulfills certain formulas. I have tried in my writing to avoid stereotypes as far as I understood them and to tell what I knew and to present people by not writing down about them. I think that's apt to be less popular, at least immediately, and it's harder to do. We like to read about things very different from our experience. Somebody sitting in the suburbs and in the university enjoys reading something really exotic and grotesque. The word *novel* means something new and different. I had never thought of the term *Appalachian* really until in the mid-to late seventies. I originally said "mountain people." *Appalachian* is not a term we used very much. I guess the best answer is that my writing is Appalachian because the setting is there; beyond that I would find it very hard to identify motifs and patterns that make something specifically Appalachian.

WH: The questioner sounds kind of skeptical, even resentful, about what the term *Appalachian* had been turned into.

Q: Much of the notion of *Appalachian* is created from outside. Part of the problem is in trying to define who we are in relation to a national image. I have a problem with writing as nostalgia, without a vision of the future.

RM: But can you think of any great creative writing that envisions the future that way? There's a passage in Shelley's "Defense of Poetry" where he talks about what he calls the moral imagination, and he lists the great writers he thinks have the moral imagination. Then he says there's a lesser kind of poet. Now Shelley was an activist, a political poet, a radical poet. He says there's a lesser kind of poet who tries to address issues directly; he does not recreate his world. Shelley thinks that is a lesser kind of poetry. I think most current political issues can be addressed more effectively in speeches and editorials and by getting out in the picket line than in a poem that might be read by about fifty people—if you're lucky. Language is by its own nature narrative. When you get up and start telling people a story, you say "this happened," not "this is going to happen." And they want to know what happened. I don't think language was invented by people for utilitarian purposes primarily, but as a medium of delight. When you got back from the buffalo hunt, you said, "I saw this big thing, it was really big, and I chased it," and everybody was listening.

WH: Is that more true of the southern or mountain or Appalachian spirit?

RM: No, I think it's in every culture and every people. We are closer to it because we have not been as urbanized and perhaps have not been reading as long. People closer to the oral tradition are usually the better storytellers. New England had all these schools and educated preachers while people in this part of the world had a tradition of Baptist preachers who were not so schooled but were wonderful users of rhetoric and improvisation. Our tradition is that, and frontier humor—the tall tale, which is a thing that Mark Twain used and other writers like Faulkner. But people in other parts of the country and other cultures have just as much trouble identifying what is really definitive. Nobody in New England can agree on what is really New England; they can't agree on what is really Massachusetts culture. Eudora Welty said one of the most interesting things I've heard about the mountains. Her mother came from West Virginia and in her book *One Writer's Beginnings*, she talks about going back to West Virginia with her mother and discovering the peculiar combination of sentiment and fear that the mountain people have.

I once came across a word in Welsh, *hiraeth*. It means an intense longing for home, which Welsh people are supposed to feel—or Celtic people. Most of the people from my part of the mountains are of Welsh ancestry: Thomas, Morgan, Powell. But there's no such thing as pure Appalachian. Let me give you an example. I had a cousin—my father's second cousin—who grew up on Green River where I did, and at the turn of the century he went off to Wake Forest and worked his way through Wake Forest College. He was in the army in World War I. He went on to Cornell and then attended Harvard, and he got a doctorate in engineering from the Sorbonne. That's somebody from Green River, you know. So you could say, "No, none of your family had any formal education." But there are

always exceptions to any generalization. It's pretty hard to make a statement and have it apply everywhere. I knew other people who were educated even though they never left the farm.

Something that I have identified in my own writing, after the fact, is a
pattern of people trying to escape the mountains. I've discovered that many
of the stories that I have written are about people, even back into the nineteenth century, who were trying to escape the walls of the mountains to go
to Charleston, or Columbia, or Raleigh, to get away, and almost invariably
coming back because some invisible tether pulled them back. I know in
my own family, my uncles moved away and then returned, except the one
who was killed in World War II. My dad tried to leave the mountains
several times to be a trapper in Canada, to go to Minnesota and raise
wheat, but he always came back. It's very hard to escape that repulsion
and attraction.

Q: Do you write poetry and fiction for an ideal reader?

RM: I think maybe different works are for different people. Insofar
as I visualize a reader, I try to write for somebody smarter than I am—
somebody who can pick up very quickly what I'm getting at. I try not to
write down to people. I think you should write up to people, assume that
they're more intelligent and much better read, and make the writing as
sophisticated and as true as you can.

WH: Is the audience for a poem restricted?

RM: It's bigger than Donne's audience. Poetry has never needed a big
audience. It's the one literary art that can thrive almost in solitude. Some
of our greatest poets, both in England and in America, have written for
tiny audiences, often seemingly for no audience at all. Dickinson is probably the greatest American poet. She showed her poems to about a half
dozen people; she published nine anonymously in her life. Stevens until he
was middle-aged was known to very few people, and many people consider
him the greatest American poet of the twentieth century. Hardy was famous for his novels and nobody much liked his poems. You can't imagine
novels being written for a tiny audience or for no audience. Short stories
were developed in magazines and were a child of journalism. The novel
developed in the eighteenth century for the middle-class reader—the newly
literate middle-class reader. Poetry is primeval. You can't find a language
or culture that doesn't have it. It just seems to be the essence of language.
Emerson said, "Every word is a fossil poem."

But I don't think you need a big audience. You don't need prizes. You don't need popularity as a writer. In fact, it may be more satisfying to write almost in private. I think the luckiest poets perhaps are those who have a devoted small audience. For a long time I did not give readings because I thought my poems did not sound like they were for a big audience. I thought they had been written in solitude and they should be read in solitude. It was only after I went off to Cornell and started to write longer, more conversational, narrative poems, that I began to feel comfortable reading them before audiences.

WH: We have a quarter of a billion people in this country, and the successful book of poetry may sell no more than a couple of thousand copies.

RM: There's a wonderful audience for poetry. I have had such great experiences at different places, giving readings and meeting people. There are readers. They like poetry. Sometimes we wish that poetry sold like Judith Krantz. Then you could live on the royalties.

Q: You once talked about the need to get out from under Calvinism, yet yesterday in a class meeting you said there was no such thing as secular poetry. Would you comment on that?

RM: I don't think there's any doubt that it's relevant that I grew up in a fundamentalist church and heard the language of the Bible and the language of preachers; and perhaps more important was being among people who thought of things in spiritual terms—moral and spiritual terms. I can't imagine poetry without some sense of worlds beyond the merely physical; perhaps poetry is the unifier, seeing at once the spiritual and the physical. As Emerson said in the last paragraph of his essay "The Poet," "The ideal shall be real to thee." The great poets like Milton, Dante, and Virgil talk about the interaction of the divine world and the world of time. A poet like Walt Whitman begins great American poetry with some sort of revelation—we don't know the nature of it, but it seems to have been some kind of radical visitation.

One of the great surprises to me in going back through my notebooks to edit my selected poems was to discover that almost all of my better poems were written in one draft. I've been teaching for twenty years and telling students how important revisions, hard work and patience are. But most of the poems I consider my best poems came all at once and were written virtually intact in the first draft. There really is such a thing as inspiration. You never know when you can write a poem and you never know if you can do it again. Roethke said that after he wrote a good poem, he got down on his knees and prayed that he could do it again. One of the pleasures of writing fiction is that it's given to you everyday to get up and work for a few hours. With poetry, it either comes or it doesn't. A poem is a gift.

Q: You discovered the influence of your father and grandfather. I wonder about the influence of women on your work.

RM: I think that most male poets are very much influenced by their mothers and most women poets are very much influenced by their fathers. Dickinson would be the type of that; she was very close to her father and she had his gift of language, colorful rhetoric, intellectual authority. I have actually written more about women than most people seem to realize. There are a lot of poems about my grandmother Levi, one about my great-grandmother Capps called "White Autumn," and "Halley's Comet" about my grandmother Morgan. Much of my fiction is about women and spoken by women. I've often found it easier to write a story if I put it in the mouth of a woman character. In some cases, very old women looking back on their lives. I've recently written a novella about a woman in her seventies who has just had a leg amputated and she's sitting in a rest home remembering her life. Once I hear the voice, I can just go with it. I sort of sit and listen and write it down. But I can't explain why I've written more about women in prose than in poetry. In some cases I don't want to know too much about what I'm doing. As long as it's working, I go with it.

WH: Let me conclude by speaking for everybody here and telling you how much we love and appreciate and praise what you have done. We hope you continue for a long time.

RM: It has been a great honor.